RAILWAY
ODDITIES

RAILWAY ODDITIES

GEOFFREY BODY

TEMPUS

First published 2007

Tempus Publishing
Cirencester Road, Chalford,
Stroud, Gloucestershire, GL6 8PE
www.tempus-publishing.com

Tempus Publishing is an imprint of NPI Media Group

British Library Cataloguing in Publication Data.
A catalogue record for this book is available from the British Library.

ISBN 978 0 7524 4399 7

Typesetting and origination by NPI Media Group
Printed in Great Britain

CONTENTS

	Introduction, Sources and Acknowledgements	6
One	Lines of Character	7
Two	Passenger Travel	19
Three	Freight Traffic	31
Four	Animals and Birds	40
Five	Best-Laid Plans	48
Six	Unusual Systems	56
Seven	Unusual Operation	64
Eight	Enterprise	73
Nine	Drama	80
Ten	Barely Believable	90
Eleven	Stations and Depots	100
Twelve	Jobs and People	110
Thirteen	Control	118
Fourteen	Traction	123
Fifteen	Comedy and Characters	135
Sixteen	Word Power	147
Seventeen	The Railway Language	154
Eighteen	Ancillary Activities	162
Nineteen	Byways	169
Twenty	Looking Back	176
Twenty-one	Just Different	184

INTRODUCTION, SOURCES AND ACKNOWLEDGEMENTS

Much has been written about railway history, operation and equipment but less about the more human side of this great industry. Yet it has always had intriguing and out-of-the-ordinary features in plenty, revealed in the enterprise, imagination and humour of its staff, the byways explored by its promoters, engineers and operators and the unusual and dramatic situations that were bound to occur over two centuries of constant and widespread activity. Based on the author's own varied railway career, the many tales generously contributed by friends and colleagues and the incredible wealth of railway writings, this book attempts to portray a somewhat different, sometimes extreme, frequently humorous, and certainly very human face of the railway industry.

In addition to the material drawn from the national and railway press and from the vast range of railway books, the author owes a great debt to the many friends, some no longer with us, who have so willingly supplied anecdotes from their own careers and experience; especially to David Ainsworth, Trevor and Diane Anderson, Ian Body, Bill Bradshaw, Jim Burnham, Charles Clinker, John Cormack, Roy Gallop, Hugh Jenkins, Stan Judd, Roger Lacy, Fernley Maker, Ray Manners, Peter Nicholls, Bob Poynter, Harold Redmile and Harold Tippler. Apart from those kindly supplied by British Rail and the Docklands Light Railway, the illustrations are drawn from the author's own collection, built up in the course of some sixty years of working for, photographing and writing about railways.

In addition to his own twenty-seven-year railway career, the author's father, wife and son all worked in the industry. This book is intended as a small tribute to them and to all railwaymen for the constant evidence of their dedication, professionalism and good humour over the best part of two centuries.

ONE

LINES OF CHARACTER

Every railway ever built had its own special character; some had – and others still have – rather more 'special character' than might be considered normal. Of course, modernisation and rationalisation have taken their toll but it is still possible to enjoy a notable travel experience on one of the 'Great Little Trains of Wales' or over scenic routes like the Settle & Carlisle, the West Highland or the Devon coastal stretch through Dawlish.

Many of the earlier railways had their own eccentricities as a result of promoters and builders providing inventive solutions to problems of terrain, traffics or finance. Highly individual industrial lines abounded, some underground and some with steep inclines, while at the other end of the spectrum there were lines like the Wissington Light Railway which wandered around the Norfolk fens to bring a few wagons of farm produce to the main line. Such lines and the passenger-carrying lines built under Light Railway Orders were often notable for the variety of their hand-me-down locomotives and rolling stock.

Weston's First Railway

When the first section of the Bristol & Exeter (B&E) Railway's main line was opened between Bristol and Bridgwater on 14 June 1841 it passed inland of the small but growing Somerset coastal resort of Weston-super-Mare, partly due to the cost and difficulties of acquiring land in the area. Instead, a short single line was built from a junction on the main line to a modest station situated where Weston's floral clock later stood. Connections with the main line trains were provided by a horse-worked branch train more notable for character than for speed, reliability or comfort.

The branch 'train' consisted of three light four-wheeled coaches provided with toast rack seats, but with little else in the way of comfort. It was hauled by three horses in tandem, with a lad in charge of each. The animals were not always in prime condition and their riders were not especially skilled or dedicated.

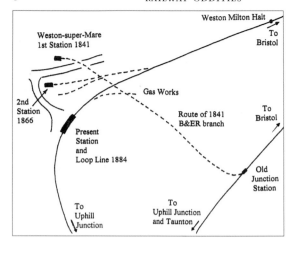

Map showing the development of the railways of Weston-super-Mare.

Speeds rarely exceeded 2mph especially if there was a head wind, and some local passengers found that they could walk the 1.5-mile route more quickly!

There was no choice but to complete the journey on foot when one of the horses drawing an evening train from Weston to the junction in 1847 succumbed to a diseased heart and collapsed on the line. The following coaches passed over the unfortunate animal and became derailed, leaving their shaken passengers to make their way forward as best they could. A subsequent 'memorial' to the railway directors resulted in the morning Bristol express and its evening counterpart being locomotive-hauled throughout from the beginning of 1848, but the other eight daily trains each way remained in the hands of the horses and horse boys.

Matters then got worse. Nine days into 1849 the rear animal of the train due in Weston at 5.45 p.m. fell, had its feet severed and had to be put down. In November the leading horse of a train fell and had its head cut off, its rider having one leg run over and the other trapped under his steed. Two horses suffered in the following month when the front horse fell and had its back broken after being struck by the leading coach, the second horse being knocked down and injured. More mishaps followed in 1850.

In an endeavour to solve the problems of the Weston–super–Mare branch the B&E tried out a steam-powered coach from Fairfields of Bow but it was not a complete success and conventional haulage took over all the branch trains from April 1851.

Seven Miles of Marshes

Marshy areas were a problem for railways right from the difficulties encountered by the pioneer Liverpool & Manchester Railway in crossing Chat Moss, a huge and deep bog lying between Patricroft and Glazebury. Not only did such areas of waterlogged ground present problems of track stability but they were usually sparsely populated as well and offered little in the way of traffic that would contribute to the higher-than-normal construction costs.

There is a reminder of this in one of the most curious of railway survivals, the long and lonely single line that accompanies the River Yare across Reedham Marshes in Norfolk. Running from Reedham to Breydon Junction near Great Yarmouth, the once-generous service of thirteen trains a day has now dropped to four on weekdays. However, for the tiny community using the intermediate station at Berney Arms, far from normal roads, they are extremely important.

The line was opened by the Yarmouth & Norwich (Y&N) Railway on 1 May 1844 but, even then, traffic to and from Berney Arms was so sparse that the Eastern Counties Railway (ECR), successor to the Y&N, stopped serving it in 1850. Mr Berney had originally sold the land on the understanding that a station would be provided in perpetuity, but the agreement omitted to require that trains stop there. Ten years of negotiation and litigation ensued before judgement was given in Berney's favour, although the ECR had restored the service in 1855.

A more direct route to Yarmouth was opened via Acle in 1883, further isolating Berney Arms. However, the tallest windmill in Norfolk was built there. This was not for use as a drainage mill but to power a cement factory which received its raw materials and distributed its finished products by Norfolk sailing wherries. Even after that activity had long gone, trains continued to traverse this unusual marsh route, dramatic and desolate in winter gales but with a rare, natural beauty in the summer months.

Feudal Railway

The aristocracy had a big influence on our railway system, some of it good and some not so good. Some noblemen helped in the promotion of new lines, others made good money from selling their land and a small group extorted private stations, the right to special train stops or even unnecessary cosmetic tunnelling as the price of their co-operation.

Grimsthorpe Castle in South Lincolnshire was the home of Lord Willoughby d'Eresby and provides a small example of a forward-looking nobleman's railway.

This hybrid locomotive, a traction engine design adapted for use on an industrial railway, is of the same type as the one used on Lord Willoughby's line.

When the Great Northern Railway (GNR) main line was opened north from Peterborough in 1852, passing only a few miles west of his estate, Lord Willoughby quickly saw the advantages of a link between the two. He had already experimented with steam ploughing and was soon using a steam traction engine and wagon on a timber roadway laid between the estate at Edenham and the GNR at Little Bytham. Unfortunately the steam engine was too heavy for the transverse sleepers so that some cracked, bent upwards and got entangled in the engine wheels!

Lord Willoughby knew and consulted the GWR's Daniel Gooch whose advice was to build a proper railway. This was done and worked sufficiently well for its passenger services to be shown in the Bradshaw timetables for a while, but on its noble owner's death the Edenham & Little Bytham Railway sadly went into decline. No maintenance work was done on the engines and a horse had to be used instead. When this was killed by a runaway wagon the line closed and passed into railway history.

A Rural Idyll

The lonely Lincolnshire single-line route from Bourne to Sleaford had only four trains each way in its prime and lost these as early as 1930. Freight traffic continued to be dealt with until 1964, but in later years the section of line between Billingborough and Aswarby was closed leaving the southern portion to be worked by a daily pick-up goods train from Spalding. This set out at 11.33 a.m. and took an hour to cover the 9-mile ex-Midland & Great Northern Joint Railway section to Bourne where a second brake van was added to save running round at Billingborough, which was reached at 3 p.m. after another 9 miles and dropping off wagons at the stations en route. An hour was allowed for the shunting work at the end of the line, after which the train picked up loaded wagons on its way back through Rippingale and Morton Road. All the outwards consignments were marshalled for easy transfer to the evening freight departures from Spalding, which was reached at 5.45 p.m.

Although the engine and footplate crew changed weekly, the 'Billingborough Goods' job was always worked by the same guard with the same brake van. He had some help from what station staff remained but otherwise did all the shunting and opening of crossing gates. The job was not a sinecure but it was regular, predictable and largely free from supervision.

Occasionally another railwayman might travel on the train and discover that this was a very different and personal world. The guard's van was the best that could be hand-picked from those working in the Spalding yard and, when unlocked, its interior presented the appearance of a gypsy living van. There were curtains, plenty of lamps, a radio and a water jug and basin. The polished black stove was fed from a shining brass coal scuttle full of the best engine coal and a fine kettle permanently simmered on the top, ready to fill the china teapot nearby. The guard was a serious pipe smoker who had fixed up a rack for a selection of favourite pipes, which he rotated with others hanging on an apple tree in his garden to sweeten. Another rack was for his guns, 12-bore, .22 sporting rifle and the like.

On the lonely Bourne to Billingborough section, with empty fens on one side and gentler pastures on the other, the whole crew co-operated to make enough time out of the running to bag a few rabbits or pigeons for the pot and to garner mushrooms, blackberries or whatever natural bounty was in season. Any surplus would be exchanged for vegetables with friendly lineside dwellers, all in an atmosphere of the greatest goodwill. If the visiting railwayman found all this eye-opening, it was also very warm and natural and, as the job was never allowed to suffer, entirely excusable. Perhaps, among the legion of railway ghosts, an ephemeral train can still be seen at dusk on the old Billingborough route, its brake van full of light, music and the smell of food on the glowing stove.

The Golden Mile

When Sir Charles Morgan agreed to lease out some land he owned near the ironworks in the Sirhowy Valley and his home at Tredegar Park he began a process that would make him very rich. To provide an outlet from the area to Newport and the Bristol Channel, an Act of 1802 allowed the Sirhowy Tramroad Co. to build a plateway to meet a similar tramroad which, with the Tredegar Park portion, completed the route into Newport. A condition of allowing the new line to pass through Sir Charles's estate on the approaches to Newport was the right to collect tolls of one penny per ton per mile on all the traffic it carried.

Few could have imagined how profitable this proviso was to prove. By the 1830s the income from the toll was averaging £10,000 a year, a very great sum for those days. The demand for coal increased year by year too, with the toll payments following suit. It continued to rise as the railways working over the 'Park Mile' increased to four and the number of tracks to six. No wonder people began to call it the Golden Mile. The GWR eventually bought out the tolls in 1923.

The Medallion

The West of England divisional manager visited all his stations as often as other duties would permit but could not get to some of the more isolated places very often. However, at last an opportunity arose for himself and his commercial manager to make a trip on the diesel multiple unit that operated the short run from the Weymouth line junction at Maiden Newton to the terminus at Bridport, a very rural branch line on which nothing out of the ordinary ever happened. The staff were all regulars, the passengers all friends and the whole operation clearly had an informality only to be found on lines remote from authority.

Unannounced, these top railway officers joined the train like ordinary passengers and, very properly but probably unusually, were asked by the conductor guard to show their tickets. He was so impressed by the commercial manager's 'All Stations' pass that he called the driver and other passengers over to inspect it. The silver medallion that entitled the divisional manager to travel anywhere at anytime should have been even more impressive but instead provoked the comment, 'That's nice, what did you win it for? And why haven't you got an 'All Stations' pass like him?'

The Marquis of Exeter's Railway

The Great Northern Railway's choice of a route through Peterborough for its main line from London to York was soon seen as putting its older neighbour, Stamford, at a serious disadvantage. Within two years of opening the first section of the new trunk route Stamford interests had lodged plans at the Board of Trade for a 3.6-mile branch line to connect with it at Essendine. The biggest shareholder in this modest enterprise was the second Marquis of Exeter, who was to have a major influence on its character.

The headquarters of the Stamford & Essendine (S&E) Railway was incorporated into its Stamford terminus, which was provided with a dramatic station building constructed in Tudor style, using local stone and to a design that clearly reflected that of the nearby Burleigh House, home of the Marquis. Inside, an atmospheric square booking hall was lit by a lantern roof, with the rooms at first-floor level linked by a walkway supported by ornate brackets and edged by decorative ironwork. Back at ground level doors led to the central platform and two platform lines beneath an overall roof.

From its opening in 1856 the GNR worked the daily branch service of four trains each way until the beginning of 1865 when the *Railway Times* announced:

The former Stamford East station offices later became a private dwelling but, despite losing some of the original architectural embellishments, remained an attractive building.

Like many
stations with
'Road' in their
name, Wansford
Road station
was a long way
from anywhere,
a feature still
apparent even
thirty-two years
after its last train.

The Marquis of Exeter, as principal proprietor of this short line, has taken the
working of it into his own hands. The Marquis has purchased new rolling stock
and has commenced running the trains with officials of his own appointment,
the agreement with the Great Northern for the working of the line having
expired. The first class carriages now bear the coat of arms of the Marquis.

His coat of arms also appeared on the front of the station and there is a suggestion
that the passenger guards on the line wore the livery of the Marquis.

The junction of the line at Essendine was the wrong way round to permit
through running to London and coal brought in this way proved no cheaper
than that via the Midland Railway route to Stamford. To remedy this the
S&E obtained an Act for a second line to the south to meet the London
& North Western Railway at Wansford. Again the junction was made the
wrong way round and traffic proved so sparse that closure occurred as early
as 1929, after just sixty-two years of eccentric life.

Known variously as the 'Pig and Whistle' or the 'Bread and Onion', the
8.5-mile branch was worked by a one engine and coach set that, prior to
closure, only managed three daily trips each way. These did not begin until
the 10.35 a.m. departure from Stamford and ended with an arrival back there
at 7.18 p.m., the guard having extinguished the station oil lamps after each
call. A legend that at one time the line had been supervised by the Stamford
stationmaster on horseback seems eminently believable.

Throughout their working life the Stamford branches certainly exhibited
character. The tank engines that worked the trains gave the author his first
footplate experience but, fortunately, not back in July 1878 when 0-4-2

saddle tank No.503 managed to derail itself by the bridge over the River Welland on the approach to Stamford and plunged, along with a truck of lime, into the waters below. It was recovered, minus its chimney, and soon became known as 'The Welland Diver' in local circles. Around this period trains arriving at Stamford halted at a ticket platform and were then rope-hauled into the station by the train engine, which had moved to a parallel line. It all went wrong on one occasion around 1896 when the coaches were not braked sufficiently and crashed through the end buffers. The GNR had to pay out a large sum in compensation and provide separate platforms and a signal box to ensure there was no repeat of this accident.

Although passenger services ceased to use Stamford East in 1957 a goods service was provided to its Priory Sidings for another ten years. This meant retaining the signal box, which was a sizeable structure backing on to the river. Its entrance lobby at the top of the steps made a fine platform for a bit of angling when there were no trains about, a practice entirely in keeping with the relaxed atmosphere of this delightful piece of railway.

The Only Underground Cable Railway in the World

This was the claim of the Glasgow District Subway, whose other slogans included 'No Smoke, No Steam, Perfect Ventilation' and 'No Need for Time Tables, Trains every few Minutes, with Perfect Regularity'. Their justification lay in the fact that the 6.55-mile 'circular' route was opened as a cable-operated line powered by two stationary steam engines. The opening day in 1896 involved two accidents – one injuring a number of passengers – but the cable and steam combination then worked well enough until electrification was completed in 1935.

The 'Subway', as it was always known, had a lot of character. Its publicity reference to 'Roomy and Commodious Cars' was true only by the standards of the day, for they were limited by the 4ft gauge. Access from narrow platforms was via 'concertina' gates to longitudinal wooden seats lit by a pick-up electric system, which produced constant flickering. The company built a dramatic turreted edifice at its main St Enoch station, but elsewhere entrances tended to be through any building handy to the route.

In order to maintain the modest dividends economy was the watchword, especially as competition from surface trams increased, and one money-saving measure used was to line and varnish carriages only on the side visible to passengers. The system also had a curious arrangement of running a special train after the end of normal services to collect the ticket takings from each station and convey them to Govan.

The subway was totally reconstructed in the 1970s and reopened in 1980 when it acquired the affectionate label of the 'Clockwork Orange'.

'To Services of Minstrels…'

Having an exclamation mark included in its title was not the only thing which made the Bideford, Westward Ho! & Appledore (BWH!&A) Railway different. Among others was the regular appearance in its traffic expenses account of a sum paid out for the 'Services of Minstrels'. This was because the small Devon line was part of the giant British Electric Traction group which was known for encouraging imaginative efforts to stimulate traffic and had provided a concert hall adjacent to Westward Ho! station as a venue for seaside entertainers. The railway also offered special 'bathing return' tickets, as well as the more usual cheap market day fares.

Single with passing loops, the 7-mile BWH!&A ran west from Bideford Quay to the coast, which it then followed northwards to Westward Ho! before turning inland again to Northam and Appledore. It was opened to Northam in 1901 and extended to Appledore in 1908, but then lasted only until 1917 when it was requisitioned by the Government and never reopened. In its short life the BWH!&A crammed in major legal battles with both its contractor and with Bideford Council.

The railway, having no turntable, ran its three Hunslet 2-4-2T locomotives for the whole of their lives with two of them facing one way and one the other. They were used with rather grand bogie coaches, one at a time mostly, with end verandahs and highly ornate furnishings. The polished teak exterior was ornamented with the company's lengthy title with the Bideford coat of arms beneath. The BWH!&A did carry a little coal transferred from coastal vessels discharging at Bideford Quay but not much else in the way of goods traffic. Here, again, it chose to be different in that its wagons were provided only with a single central buffer

Despite its promotional efforts this little line was just too circuitous to survive, but the company itself was still extant in 1922 when its records showed that the capital expenditure had totalled £67,992 and also included the telling phrase 'No dividend has yet been paid'. Bradshaw timetables at that time still included the BWH!&A but with the comment 'Service Suspended'. This could have been considered over-optimistic as the locomotives seem to have disappeared after their service in France and the carriages were sold off in 1921, one at least being converted into a beach hut.

0-6-0 ST locomotive No.2196 *Gwendraeth* was built in 1906 and needed a cut-down cab because of height restrictions on the line.

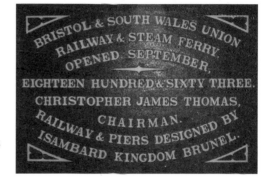

This large iron plaque on Bristol Temple Meads station pays tribute to the 1863 creation of a new route to South Wales to avoid the circuitous journey via Gloucester.

BRISTOL & SOUTH WALES UNION
RAILWAY & STEAM FERRY.
OPENED SEPTEMBER,
EIGHTEEN HUNDRED & SIXTY THREE.
CHRISTOPHER JAMES THOMAS,
CHAIRMAN.
RAILWAY & PIERS DESIGNED BY
ISAMBARD KINGDOM BRUNEL.

Prior to the opening of the Severn Tunnel passengers who had travelled down from London during the day could stay at the New Passage Hotel before continuing their journey by ferry steamer in the morning.

Burry Port & Gwendraeth Valley Railway

The Burry Port & Gwendraeth Valley (BP&GV) Railway opened its line to
Cwmmawr in 1869 by making use of some of the earthworks and structures
of Wales's first canal. It paid a penalty for this in restrictive clearances beneath
bridges along the route. The railway was also 'different' in several other ways.
It spent some of its early years in the hands of a receiver but then paid
regular dividends of 10 per cent when the market for Cwmmawr anthracite
improved. It operated double-ended Fairlie locomotives at one period and
at another had a chairman with a treble-barrelled name, Colonel Sir Thomas
E. Milborne-Swinnerton-Pilkington. Some years before the introduction of
a conventional passenger service the BP&GV agreed to provide a workmen's
service by hauling colliery-owned coaches at 50s per coach per week, and
allowed miners' wives to use them for free on payment of sixpence for each
shopping basket carried. This highly individual 21-mile railway had its own
dock, power station and workshops.

Two Tier Main Line

Prior to the opening of the Severn Tunnel in 1886, the shortest route
between Bristol and South Wales involved taking the train to New Passage
on the Gloucestershire side of the Severn Estuary and then a steam ferry
over to Portskewett on the Welsh side. The 11.5-mile single line of the
Bristol & South Wales Union (B&SWU) Railway had been opened in 1863
to a pier at New Passage where the passengers transferred to pontoons for
their steamer journey. The GWR took over the line in 1868 and later, as
part of the creation of a new through route via the tunnel, doubled the line
to Pilning Junction and closed the end section of the old B&SWU from
there to the ferry.

   The additional line at Patchway was constructed to an easier gradient of
1 in 100 and given a separate tunnel exactly a mile long, plus the 62-yard
Patchway Short Tunnel. The old tunnel on the Down line is 1,246 yards long
but has a gradient of 1 in 68, so that the two lines, although close together,
run at different heights, a noticeable disparity for a main line route. Another
curiosity is that part of the old Pilning–New Passage line was reopened in
1900 to link with the Bristol–Avonmouth branch and thus create a circular
route and a new train service round north-west Bristol.

TWO

PASSENGER TRAVEL

The first railways were built to carry merchandise – coal to the seaports, cotton to the mills and other bulk commodities for which canal transport was both limited and slow. Passengers were something of an afterthought and the pioneer Stockton & Darlington (S&D) Railway thought so little of them that it initially allowed contractors to run their own passenger service in between the company's mineral trains. The S&D soon realised that there was money to be made from carrying passengers but, even so, most of the early railways assumed that only the gentry would be able to afford train travel.

Provision for upper class travellers in the early years was lavish, with carriages designed by coach builders and allowances made for moving servants, horses and the whole entourage of the rich. Any provision for the 'lower classes' tended to be in open wagons with spartan seating and confined to slower trains. Then, given a boost by Thomas Cook's early excursions, the idea of catering for a wider travel market gradually caught on until railways were displaying great imagination in their efforts to earn more money from fares. As competition from road transport increased railways responded with an incredible variety of ideas for protecting passenger revenue, which was eventually to exceed that from freight.

Class Distinction

The early railways made their attitude to the various classes of passenger very clear. The London & Birmingham explained that its First Class Trains were made of up of carriages 'carrying Four inside (one compartment of which is convertible into a Bed Carriage, if required) and of carriages carrying Six inside'. Mixed Trains also included Second Class Carriages, 'open at the side, without linings, cushions or divisions in the compartments'.

Servants in livery could travel in the front compartment of First Class Trains on the Grand Junction Railway but ordinary people were just not expected to travel and the Great Western made it clear that it would carry certain passengers 'in uncovered trucks by Goods Train only'.

The First Excursion

The 1834 Bodmin & Wadebridge Railway (B&WR) was a remarkable enterprise, not least because it anticipated Thomas Cook's famous Leicester–Loughborough excursion by several years. When its locomotives *Elephant* and *Camel* set off from Wadebridge for Wenford Bridge on 14 June 1836 with some 800 passengers they achieved the distinction of working the country's first cheap-fare public railway excursion.

Passenger traffic was not the B&WR's main business, which was the carriage of sea sand for local farmers, but it did offer cheap day fares and was clearly alert for any revenue-earning opportunity. So much so that when William and James Lightfoot were hanged outside Bodmin Gaol in 1840 the railway immediately saw an opportunity to make money and laid on two excursions trains for the event. By today's standards such exploitation would be considered macabre, but the B&W saw it as an excellent opportunity and halted the trains at a point where the line ran near to the prison so that the passengers could watch from the comfort of their seats!

Gypsies' Warnings

The stage coach fraternity did not surrender tamely to the loss of their passengers to the early railways. After the 1843 accident at Cudworth on the North Midland Railway a poster appeared which parodied the benefits claimed for train travel assuring potential train users that not only would they get faster travel but the railway would also provide station cemeteries in which spaces could be reserved at the time of purchasing tickets!

Punch explored this theme on quite a few occasions and was still doing so in 1852 when, seeing railway accidents as inevitable, it suggested that 'a salutary dread of them should be implanted in the minds of our rising generation'. As its own contribution to the process the magazine offered four nursery rhymes. A sample verse, to be sung to the tune of 'Hush-a-by Baby', read:

> Rock away passenger in the third class,
> When your train shunts a faster will pass,
> When your train's late, your chances are small,
> Crushed will be carriages, engine and all.

Foot Warmers

A Bill before Parliament in 1850 proposed that the railways should 'supply foot-warmers, or other means of heating railway carriages in cold weather' free of charge to all passengers travelling more than 15 miles. By 1879 the GWR had the matter well in hand, sending out a supply of foot-warmers to forty-one stations on 25 October and instructing them to place one in the first and second class compartments of 'All Through and long Journey Trains'. Third class passengers were not treated quite as generously, for the Superintendent of the Line's directive continued, 'Third Class Passengers must be supplied with Warmers when they ask for them.' And not before, presumably!

Staff were told to fill the warmers with boiling water and not to heat them in front of a fire or throw them into the carriages. At night the exchange of warmers at the appointed places was to be made 'as quietly as possible in order that the passengers may not be disturbed'.

The late C. Hamilton Ellis used to tell the story of a Russian travelling in an LSWR coach which had been provided with foot-warmers. Coming from a land where anarchy and bombs were not unknown the foreigner gingerly touched the metal canister, found it suspiciously warm and promptly threw it out of the train window.

The Picnic Carriage

The idea of a tramroad from Lydney to Lydbrook, linking the Severn and Wye rivers, dates back to the end of the eighteenth century, with the Severn & Wye (S&W) Railway duly fulfilling the dream in 1810. This primitive line ran through an area well blessed with coal measures, iron ore and timber, all of which stimulated enough industry and originating freight traffic to permit the S&W to convert its tramroad to normal track standards. Later it amalgamated with the Severn Bridge Railway to obtain access to deep water shipping facilities at Sharpness on the eastern bank of the Severn.

The Severn & Wye & Severn Bridge Railway ran through some beautiful parts of the ancient Forest of Dean and the company was using posters to attract tourists to its line as early as the 1880s. Its first excursion trains offered more capacity than comfort but the potential value of tourist business, particularly in periods of industrial downturn, rapidly produced more sophisticated marketing, as the notice overleaf shows.

The picnic carriage would probably be conveyed on a regular passenger service and detached or picked up using the train engine. The locations at which it could be stabled were all in the heart of the forest, surrounded by

SEVERN & WYE & SEVERN BRIDGE RAILWAY.

FOREST OF DEAN.

Excursions, Pleasure Parties, &c., to Severn Bridge, Speech House, Lydbrook (Symonds' Yat), &c.

During the Summer Months Excursion Tickets at low fares are issued on certain Week Days (see Bills) from Midland Stations at Cheltenham, Gloucester, Bristol and Bath, to Severn Bridge, Speech House, and Lydbrook.

Cheap Return Tickets will be issued to Pleasure Parties on any day for not less than Six First Class or Ten Third Class Passengers.

An attractive Guide to the Forest of Dean has been published by Mr. JOHN BELLOWS, Gloucester, and may be had of all Booksellers.

Special Arrangements at Cheap Fares can be made for Schools, Benefit Societies, Working Men's Clubs, or Manufacturers' Annual Trips, &c.

Near the Severn Bridge Station there is Hotel accommodation and Tea Gardens overlooking the River and the Severn Bridge.

The Speech House (within a few minutes' walk of the Station) is situated on a hill in the centre of the ancient forest, and is a most attractive place for pleasure parties.

Every accommodation can be provided by the Hotel in the Speech House, or for Picnics in the open forest, and there are Cricket, Quoit, Archery, and Lawn Tennis Grounds.

Telegraphic communications to Speech House, address via Lydney.

Lydbrook is beautifully situated on the River Wye amidst charming scenery.

Symonds' Yat and Goodrich Castle are within easy walking distance from the Lydbrook Junction Station, and tickets to that Station are available to return from Coleford Station, or vice versa.

A Picnic Carriage for Parties of about a dozen can be provided on application to the General Manager, Lydney. The charge for the carriage, in addition to the first class fare, is one guinea, which includes use of Dinner & Tea Services, Plate, Glass, Linen, and Attendant. The Carriage can be left, as desired, on Sidings near picturesque points of the forest, viz., Coleford Junction, Bixslade, Speech House Road, Serridge Junction, Drybrook Road, Lydbrook Junction.

GEO. WILLIAM KEELING,
Engineer & General Manager.

A railway notice detailing facilities for enjoying the Forest of Dean.

acres of woodland for walking off the contents of the picnic hampers laid out by the attendant. He also positioned the portable steps and made sure no one placed themselves in danger. The Speech House Hotel referred to in the notice was the traditional meeting place for the Free Miners of the Forest and of the courts by which the forest law was administered.

A Stop at Llandod

In the heyday of the British spas, Llandrindod Wells – locally referred to as Llandod – attracted around 80,000 visitors in a typical season. Most came by train and the town's station on the Central Wales Line enjoyed through carriages to and from London, Birmingham, Liverpool and Manchester. The spa visitors were not the type to travel light or to be overly concerned about railway punctuality and so very few trains stopped for only their booked time.

The number of hotel porters meeting arriving trains grew steadily from around five to nearer thirty as the resort grew in popularity. Many wore smart uniforms trimmed with gold and each believed his guests' luggage should be first out of the luggage vans. The resultant jostling, noise and confusion from this large throng could easily defeat the efforts of the stationmaster and his staff to get trains away on time, especially as the latter had their eye on the generous tips available for their services.

The upshot was that trains calling at 'Llandod' at the most popular times often took up to fifteen minutes longer than they were allowed, especially if an engine had to be worked from Builth Road to detach coaches. Since much of the Central Wales Line was single these delays had repercussions on the whole route from Craven Arms to Swansea, and the town's popularity with its visitors was not wholly shared by those who operated its railway.

Five Shillings Reward

Post-war recession and the growth of early omnibus services posed an increasing threat to poorly used railway lines in the 1920s. The eight passenger station closures in 1923 rose to fifty-five in 1929 and then to a massive 224 in 1930, a figure that was not then to be exceeded until 1950. One of the early attempts to improve the profitability of rural lines had resulted in the introduction of steam railcars in the mid-1920s; the LNER tested its Sentinel-Cammell cars on the East Yorkshire lines and then extended their use to Scotland and eastern England. By 1930 there were seventy-seven steam railcars in service, their running costs proving about half those incurred with other options for reducing operating costs, such as the use of auto-trains which could be driven from either end.

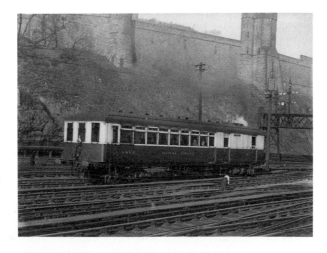

The steam railcar *Royal Eagle* near Edinburgh Waverley station.

The LNER railcars were named after former stage coaches and each displayed details of the route and journeys of its namesake. An internal circular of July 1928 recorded:

> Steam Rail cars named after the Old Stage Coaches i.e. 'Transit', Chevy Chase'. Railway' and 'Bang-Up' will shortly be put into working. A framed notice is exhibited in each car giving full particulars of the Old Stage Coach after which the car is named, and offering a reward of 5/- to anyone who can supply to any L.N.E.R. station master hitherto unpublished information relating to the Old Stage Coaches in question.

The Club Car

Those who use trains a lot get quite knowledgeable about them and quite skilled in ways of making their journeys as comfortable as possible. This factor, together with the efforts of the railways to provide inducements to increase the number of clients making regular journeys, led to the old Lancashire & Yorkshire Railway coming up with the idea of treating groups of the wealthy businessmen who regularly commuted into Manchester as a club which enjoyed special privileges.

The provision of a separate carriage for members of a travelling club between Blackpool and Manchester dates back to around 1896. Regular travellers from Llandudno and Windermere subsequently came to enjoy similar facilities which, in return for the payment of a supplement and a club membership fee, in addition to the first class contract ticket fare, provided exclusive use of a club coach on the principal morning and evening express commuter train. The design of these coaches varied over the years but would typically involve first class compartments plus an open saloon area with comfortable individual chairs. There were lavatory facilities and an attendant to look after the cloakroom and serve refreshments; all this for a typical subscription of around five guineas a year. Each club member received in return a membership folder issued by the railway and the club secretary.

In the manner of such things each club member tended to have his own favourite seat and for anyone else to usurp this was extremely bad form. They were watchful of the timekeeping of their trains, keeping an eye on the carriage clock, and were quick to comment if things went wrong. Stationmasters, footplatemen and signalmen all needed to ensure priority for the club trains or explain themselves to higher authority if anything went wrong. One story is told of a club which had its own thermometer in the train to ensure the steam heating provided a comfortable temperature on cold mornings, but there were occasions when potential critics might need to be detained in conversation while the platform inspector applied a match to the bulb of the thermometer to provide an acceptable reading!

The club tradition ended in the early years of the Second World War but groups of regular travellers with favourite seats will always be a feature of certain trains and routes.

For a Small Extra Charge

Prior to 1 July 1904, when the Cornish Riviera included a dining car for the first time, train guards were able to take and telegraph forward orders for a 2s 6d luncheon or refreshment basket to be provided at one of the main stations along the line. Extras available included a small bottle of claret for 1s 3d or a bottle of beer for 6d. First class passengers could also hire a small folding table for 6d.

Commuting Skills

If there was a Society of Advanced Commuters its members would display skills such as Precise Platform Positioning. This is the art of being in exactly the right spot to nip quickly onto the incoming train and secure a favourite seat. Among a whole host of other skills would be broadsheet newspaper

A 1907 comic postcard view of rail travel.

management or staying asleep until the final approach to one's destination. The talents of reading, conversation, computing and people watching would all be characteristics of society members.

For many years around the 1950s there was a five-something evening service from King's Cross to Peterborough and Cambridge. The train would be double-headed by two locomotives on the first part of its journey, usually with a 4-4-0 Claud as train engine on the front Cambridge section and a B1 4-6-0 acting as pilot. On arrival at Hitchin the group of regulars heading for the stations further along the main line would alight from the rear part of the train, hasten to the refreshment room and order their tea, coffee or whatever. The refreshment room staff were ready so this was all achieved while the pilot engine was uncoupled and moved forward. By this time the commuters from the rear coaches, warm drinks in hand, were grouped around the cheery coal fire. The Claud locomotive then left for Cambridge with its half train, signalling that it was the time for the tea drinkers to leave the warm fire and rejoin their carriages as the B1 set back onto its half. On the resumed journey, at least one of the group, whose home was only a couple of fields away from the Biggleswade to Sandy portion of the main line, would use the compartment light switch to signal 'Turn up the oven, Love, I shall be home shortly'!

Holiday Routes to the West

The heavy Summer Saturday traffic to the west of England was always a great challenge for the two great main lines that carried it. That doyen of

Crowds wait to join the train of empty coaches arriving at No.1 platform at Paddington.

the southern route via Salisbury, the Atlantic Coast Express (ACE), ran to thirteen coaches and nine portions even in winter and needed four separate trains on Saturdays in the summer. During the Second World War ACE reached a formation of sixteen coaches in ten portions, resulting in its Waterloo locomotive having to be attached at the last minute because this extra-long train prevented access to adjacent platforms.

Thousands were carried by the Great Western to and from Torbay on summer Saturdays, while its pride and joy on the main line to Cornwall was the Cornish Riviera Express. The special stock of this train ran with the corridors on the seaward side to allow holidaymakers to savour the stretch through Dawlish and Teignmouth and a major publicity impact was also achieved when the coaches were fitted with 'Vitaglass' which let the sun's rays through to give passengers an early taste of the holiday benefits to come.

Class Provision

Before railways ended the provision of second class accommodation, all three classes of travel – first, second and third – would be catered for even on even quite short trains. The same provision was also made on the single car of the GNR (Ireland)'s horse-drawn Fintona tram. Prior to the 1953 repair of the 1883 double-deck tram vehicle, damaged when the horse 'Dick' bolted, twelve first and twelve second class seats were provided in the lower saloon, and twenty-four thirds upstairs.

The Devonport Dockyard Railway went one better and, despite a route of only two miles, had five different types of accommodation on its passenger trains. Bare wood seats were provided for workmen and ratings, something slightly better for chargemen, recorders and petty officers, then better still for subordinate officers, and onwards and upwards for superior and commissioned officers, up to the ultimate blue upholstery of the 'Principal Dockyard Officers'.

Hop Pickers

Until the 1950s railways played a big part in the annual movement of labour to the hop fields of Kent and Herefordshire. During the August and September period up to 40,000 people might require movement and this figure would be swollen even further by those who came to visit them at weekends. Much care went into the train planning, but the Great Western did stipulate that 'only third class coaches of the oldest type' should be used for carrying hop pickers and the Southern Railway (SR) stored ancient non-corridor stock at Maze Hill and Blackheath for just this purpose.

In areas of London, like the East End and Elephant & Castle, there was a strong hop-picking tradition with whole families travelling to Kent, living there in wooden shacks or tents, picking the crop during the day and providing their own entertainment in the evening. From grandmother down to the youngest baby, with mattresses and other essentials loaded on a costermonger's cart, hundreds of families would trek to London Bridge station to purchase a special period ticket and have their luggage placed in the carefully labelled luggage vans. The SR worked closely with the farmers to link the labour supply with the hop ripening times and also operated a liaison office at Maidstone to control the whole operation.

The main destinations for the trains that ran from London Bridge Low Level were the main line stations between Tonbridge and Pluckley, plus the Maidstone West and Hawkhurst lines. At the start of the season up to seven trains would be required for Hawkhurst branch traffic alone, departing between 3.30 a.m. and 6 a.m. to be away before the important newspaper services from London. Each train had two guards and its users were supposed to surrender their tickets before being allowed to join. This did not always work out in practice and both travelling ticket collectors and the police had to be pretty sharp to sort out those who hid under skirts or seats screened by friendly legs or lay upon the racks beneath piles of luggage. Pulling the communication cord was an ever-present temptation and only disconnecting the vacuum and working on the engine brake alone – strictly against regulations – got some trains to their destination!

In addition to the early and late season family movements fathers came down to join in for the one week they could get off work and there were Sunday services conveying 'hop-pickers friends' for whom special tickets were also available.

Cheap Fares

Cheap rail fares were offered for parties, those with special interests like hikers or cyclists and to encourage travel to special events such as markets, agricultural shows and race meetings. Railway canvassers gave film shows to members of Women's Institutes around the country to persuade them to take an outing by rail, also screening films made by the British Transport Film Unit. From the end of the nineteenth century poster artists were commissioned to originate scenes for station display depicting alluring destinations, and millions of brochures and handbills detailing train services and special fares were distributed to stations, ticket agents and other strategic points.

Special trains were frequently run to serve London and other entertainment venues and to meet the insatiable British appetite for a holiday visit to the sea.

An invitation to take an evening trip to Southend in 1938.

Thousands were packed into Wakes Week specials to Blackpool and adjacent resorts. The WR ran preview trains to enable would-be holidaymakers to sample the resorts of Devon and Cornwall, and operated regular 'Mystery Trains' to places not publicised in advance. Low fares were available for the good people of Norwich to make an evening trip to Great Yarmouth or for Londoners to see the Southend Illuminations. The latter might even get free admission to the Kursaal fairground and gardens and there enjoy such pleasures as throwing at a target in an attempt to tip a scantily clad young lady into a tank of water.

'Like Roman Legions'

In the early years of the Glastonbury pop festival no one could have predicted that it would become so popular. The 1970 event certainly took British Rail's Western Region by surprise, with the modest extra capacity provided for intending visitors rapidly being overwhelmed. On the Friday evening before the event fans poured into Paddington 'like Roman legions' and the last train, the 23.45 to Penzance, was jam-packed despite the provision of extra coaches. Saturday was even busier with crowds of young people adding to the usual summer holiday traffic and two special trains filling up within minutes of being platformed. The group Jefferson Airplane had been refused access to the

Fans heading home from Castle Cary station after the 1970 Glastonbury pop festival.

festival site by helicopter and were pleading for BR help. A four-coach special was hurriedly assembled at Old Oak Common for the Sunday morning and the group's party allocated a coach on it but, with three Paddington booking offices being opened from 05.30 a.m., the special had grown to ten vehicles by the time it left Reading. Another special was found for hundreds of young Germans who had been stranded at Victoria. At the other end a dmu shuttle service between Bath and Castle Cary was to carry some 20,000 passengers.

Having rather more warning than the London end, the West of England Division got ready for the return rush. Staff gave up their Sunday off, windows were removed from the Castle Cary booking office to create more ticketing points, directional signs were set up and British Transport police brought in to help in marshalling BR's share of the 150,000 fans on their way from the festival site. Even so the pressure was unimaginable and needed all the skill and ingenuity of the experienced railwaymen on the spot. The Divisional Operating Manager arranged for all sorts of extra stops in passing services on the West of England main line. Empty coaching stock was grabbed if it came anywhere near and the Marketing Manager commandeered portable ticket machines and formed a mobile squad to sell tickets along the long and patient queues. For much of the period from Sunday afternoon until midday on Monday a service left Castle Cary every fifteen minutes, each train filled to capacity with music lovers.

It had all gone so well and all that remained to be done was to restore the battered station premises to some sort of order, to get hijacked locomotives, stock and people to their proper diagrams and rosters, and to account for rather a lot of cash acquired in a manner which would have had any decent railway auditor squirming!

THREE

FREIGHT TRAFFIC

The first railways had a tough job getting their schemes through Parliament, but that was only the beginning. To further protect the public interest they were regulated right from the start, one of the most onerous restrictions being the obligation as common carriers to accept and convey pretty well everything that might be offered to them. Since the rates that could be charged were also controlled the railways found themselves obliged to carry many items that involved high costs and complicated equipment or handling. The hundreds of long, slow coal trains that lumbered about the system each day were good business, but a couple of wet bags of cockles were rather less profitable.

Before the days of road transport this situation could be largely justified by the economic dependence of almost every activity on the railway freight, parcels and goods sundries network but it resulted in a business mixture that ranged from moving huge boilers to caring for live chicks.

Sea Sand Sales

The pioneer steam railway in the south-west was the Bodmin & Wadebridge (B&W) Railway which opened in 1834. Its main line ran for 12 miles from the quay at Wadebridge along the pleasant, wooded valley of the River Camel to Wenford Bridge. There were short branches to Bodmin and Ruthern Bridge.

The Bodmin & Wadebridge line was built to convey coal and sea sand inland from vessels docking at Wadebridge. The company made a handsome profit from the sand which it bought ex-ship and then resold to farmers at double the purchase price. It was such good business that the railway was able to offer an excellent service. If delivery to one of its public sidings was not convenient the B&W would arrange to stop a train at the point nearest to its client's field and for the sand to be unloaded to the trackside there; hardly something that would have been acceptable on today's busy lines. If the wagon had not been emptied within an hour a demurrage charge of £5 an hour was incurred.

Among the other unusual features of this early line was its employment of women as wharfingers.

Zulus

The ex-Highland Railway route between the Cromarty Firth on the east coast of the Highland Region of Scotland and Loch Carron on the west coast was opened by the Dingwall & Skye Railway in 1870. Built with the carriage of fish in mind, one of the original aims of the promoters had been to convey sail fishing boats, of a type known locally as 'Zulus', from one coast to the other to avoid the hazardous journey around the north of Scotland. Two 15-ton cranes were actually ordered to perform the lifts at Dingwall and Strome Ferry, and the space between the tracks at crossing points was widened to 10ft to allow trains carrying the boats to pass one another safely, but the company then had second thoughts and dropped the scheme. This was perhaps as well for the route was prone to runaway accidents and the participation of a train of fishing boats would hardly have helped its unenviable reputation.

Horse Manure

It is not something that would occur to us today but, in the era of the horse, places like cavalry barracks often produced so much manure that its disposal was a major problem. To the railway canvassers of the period, however, it was just another potential flow of traffic well anticipated in the huge goods traffic rate book.

An example was the cavalry barracks at Avonmouth, which produced multiple wagon loads of manure, all loaded by shovel, and needing to be conveyed to a suitable siding for unloading and spreading on the land. Such a siding was installed a little further south in Somerset but the loaded wagons had to be moved from Avonmouth to Bristol along one side of the Avon Gorge, go back westwards along the other to Portishead and be transferred there from the GWR sidings to those of the Weston, Clevedon & Portishead Light Railway for the final stretch to a siding at Cadbury Road Halt. Who had the unhappy job of wagon cleaning is not recorded.

Mail Cycle

Mail by rail began on the Liverpool & Manchester Railway, and the infant system soon adopted the coaching-era practice of dropping and picking it up without stopping. The Grand Junction Railway pioneered the Travelling Post Office (TPO) concept in 1838 when it built the first TPO vehicle, fitted with a simple mail exchange device. The use of lineside apparatus for mail transfers was then to last until 4 October 1971 when the West Coast Postal train dropped the final pouches just north of Penrith. So ended a system which at one time had something like 240 exchange points.

The system for transferring mail between train and lineside while on the move was essentially a simple mechanical arrangement based on suspending the bag of mail by a thick leather strap engaged by a V-shaped grip and that, in turn, triggered the release of the mail bag into a suspended net. Mostly the transfer went without a hitch but one exception did occur at Coatbridge in 1964. Well before the London–Aberdeen TPO was due there the local postman arrived for the mail exchange, leaned his bicycle against the exchange gantry beside the track and settled down to wait. What happened then is captured in a brief entry in the Perth Control log that recorded 'Frame of bicycle found in net of London TPO on arrival at Aberdeen'.

Motorail

BR's Motorail service, which carried passengers and their cars over several routes to enable holidaymakers to arrive at their destination without a tiring drive, had several predecessors. One of these was the Caledonian Railway's 'Rail Motor Service' which operated across the entrance to Loch Etive between Connel Ferry on the Oban line and Benderloch on the branch to Ballachulish. The company produced a curious looking 'car train' by converting a 30hp charabanc to carry the passengers and tow a low-sided truck on which their car could be loaded.

Although this is clearly an early car-carrying service of some sort the location of these flat wagons and the concrete access ramp and loading dock is uncertain. The cars seem to be 1930s models with the open tourer carrying its luggage behind the boot.

The Great Western also offered a car-carrying service through the Severn Tunnel, introduced to save motorists having to drive all the way up to Gloucester in order to cross the River Severn. Using loading docks at Pilning (High Level) and Severn Tunnel Junction the cars were loaded onto flat wagons and attached to local passenger trains. They had to be drained of petrol but the railway returned an equivalent amount after the journey through the tunnel.

More Cars

Back in the early 1960s very few of the cars produced at Dagenham were moved by rail. Part of the reason was that dealers bought 'ex-works' and the decision on which method of delivery should be used lay with a widely scattered group of authorised Ford agents around the country. Under the Eastern Region's first line traffic manager, J. W. Dedman, a massive campaign was mounted to see as many dealers as possible and persuade them that receiving their new cars with no mileage on the clock would be one of the several advantages of transferring their business to rail. In the course of such an errand to Plymouth the author had occasion to want to leave his suitcase on the platform for a few minutes and asked a porter if he would mind just keeping an eye on it. 'Oh, sir,' was the response. 'You must come from London. No one round here would touch your luggage.'

Of course, neither the delivery drivers nor the car transporter operators liked this railway development but it laid the groundwork for persuading Ford to take control of car delivery and pocket the savings to be made. Existing CCT wagons were used at first followed by the building of special transporter wagons. Later there were such prestige movements as the daily train loads of parts moved between the Dagenham and Halewood factories to a schedule that was an integral part of the Ford production process.

Relationships between the Ford Motor Co. and the LT&S Line railway staff were excellent but newcomers who hoped to get on well with the Ford people were, in those days, given a tour of the factory with a built-in initiation ceremony. Since both coal and pig iron were brought in by rail the foundry was part of the tour and, crossing the floor, molten ingots were skilfully skidded near enough to newcomers to test their nerve and establish their suitability for workforce approval.

Docks Traffic

Links between railways and docks go back to the very beginnings of railed movement. Many early railway schemes had the waterside as their objective

A night view of the train carrying production parts for the Ford Motor Co. passing through Barking station on its way from Dagenham to Halewood in May 1963.

although not all of them developed into the vast traffic interchange areas that characterised London, Liverpool, Southampton and others. Some of these connections live on at places like Tilbury, Felixstowe and the Southampton Maritime terminal.

Harry Kinsey often visited the London docks when he was commercial manager at Liverpool Street. An able and likeable officer, Harry had a somewhat pedantic presence which was heightened by his great command of the English language. It was totally in character for him to ask a docker where the 'urinal' was, and he was only mildly taken aback when the reply was, 'I don't know, mate. What line does she sail for?'

Some of the traffic handled by the dockers at that time was pretty horrid. The heavy, stiff and smelly hides imported for Morland's at Glastonbury certainly came in this category. Not only was handling and working docks traffic complicated but so was its documentation. Endless calculations went into making up invoices depending on what sort of wharfage, storage, handling and cartage it required. In London, for example, some traffic was unloaded overside from sea-going vessel to lighters and then transferred to rail at railway docks like Poplar or Brentford. Some went up the Regents Canal and some into warehouses on the docks or nearer London.

The original agreement between railway and dock companies at the time Tilbury was built was just one example of the complications. It involved the dock company guaranteeing a minimum annual volume of traffic in return for special rates for carrying their traffic to London and warehousing it at

To reach the quayside of the Floating Harbour at Bristol the freight line from Temple Meads had to pass over a main road, tunnel below the church of St Mary Redcliffe and then cross the entrance lock of Bathurst basin.

Commercial Road, near Fenchurch Street. At the time this all seemed a good idea and gave the more distant dock competitive access to the London area, but the penalty payment for any shortfall in the annual tonnage became a sore point as traffic levels fell in BR days. Many an acrimonious meeting took place in the Port of London Authority headquarters before agreement was finally reached on ending the arrangement.

Temple Meads Goods Depot

Goods depots handled full wagon loads in the main yard and smaller consignments in a goods shed where transfer took place between wagons and the road vehicles used for collection and delivery. The bigger depots often had many other functions as well, ranging from warehousing to cattle docks and private sidings to tenancies for coal merchants.

The largest covered railway goods shed in the world was built at Bristol by the Great Western Railway in 1926 on the site of the original 1842 shed. It was located between the passenger station and the River Avon and, together with its adjacent yard and sidings, occupied an area of over six acres. In addition to the fifteen decks inside the shed for loading and unloading sundries, there were two waterside sidings, a private siding link to Stoates Mill, and a mileage yard beside the high level route to Wapping Wharf and the Bristol Harbour lines. In addition to handling local traffic to and from the Bristol area the shed performed a major transfer function for traffic between the south-west and the rest of the country. It was a place of great activity, bustle and seeming confusion.

The interior of
the goods depot
at Bristol Temple
Meads.

Rail into Road

China clay is produced in vast quantities in the area traversed by the Par to
Newquay branch line. To move the clay, which is used for pottery, medicines
and a variety of other products, a vast network of mineral lines grew out
of two horse-worked tramways built by Squire J.T. Treffry in the 1840s. Via
the Cornwall Minerals Railway the network finally passed to the GWR,
which for years served the dozens of wharves and sidings on and linked to
the St Dennis Junction to Fowey and Burngullow through routes. In BR
days the main forwarding points were the Retew Branch, Parkandillack
and Drinnink Mill, with some of the older names like Varcoes & Goonvean
Siding, Dubbers No.1 Siding and Lukes Old Siding slowly dropping out
of use. The control point for the rail operations was St Blazey where the
locomotive shed and wagon storage sidings were also located.

So important was the china clay business to BR that negotiations with
English China Clays (ECLP) eventually led to the conversion of the
direct line from Par to Fowey into a road access route, with the rail traffic
concentrated on the Lostwithiel to Fowey branch.

Getting a Buzz

Among the more unusual railway traffics were the regular consignments
of bees forwarded from Royston station on the Hitchin–Cambridge line.
'Escapes' were not unknown and these would cause complete and utter
panic until a beekeeper could be summoned to restore order.

A wagon load of china clay has just been tipped into the hopper from which a conveyor belt will take it to the vessel loading at Fowey Harbour in 1964.

Bill Bradshaw had a similar sort of experience in the hot summer of 1965 when he was Goods Agent at Oxford. He was not overly enthusiastic about a job secured by the area salesman that involved clearing a large quantity of sugar from one of the Government buffer depots used to store strategic food supplies against the possibility of a national emergency.

The raw cane sugar, which was in 2.25cwt sacks, had to be carted into the Oxford station, but the sacks proved to be in poor condition and this was not improved by having to manhandle them. As Bill observed, 'I think that every bee and wasp in the county was in on the job, and the trailers and whole goods yard was swarming with them.' The only remedy was to rig up the depot's fire hoses and wash everything down.

After the job had at last been completed the hoses were laid out in orderly lines to dry. By a stroke of good fortune the fire inspector arrived the following morning to make an inspection, congratulated Oxford on its fire drill and gave the depot a highly favourable mention in his annual report!

The Far West

Not only is Cornwall a beautiful county but its people are delightful and full of character. From the standpoint of the railway movement of merchandise, the distances to the main markets placed growers and merchants at a cost disadvantage which dug in to the higher prices which could be obtained because the climate ripened fruit, flowers and vegetables earlier than elsewhere.

Once the early Cornish daffodils, and those shipped over from the Isles of Scilly, had been rushed to London it was time to load the heavy crops of broccoli. Growers wanted the latest possible loading times in the field and the earliest possible deliveries to Covent Garden, Nine Elms and Borough

Market. They wanted an assured supply of vans and the lowest possible rates. All this was discussed between BR staff and growers at a major pre-season meeting which, at times, got quite vocal. On one occasion – attended by the author – tempers flared up over whether the National Farmers Union members could force a better deal than the non-members, a sort of closed-shop argument. It got so heated late in the evening that the two-man railway team left them to it, their departure quite unnoticed.

Strategic matters involving rail transport occasionally called for a meeting with the chairman of Cornwall County Council. The lunch provided seemed almost a royal occasion with place cards, excellent provisions, great formality and regal service.

Great and Small

Live chicks in ventilated cardboard boxes were regularly conveyed by rail and cheeped continuously throughout their journey. As the concentration of parcels facilities proceeded, such traffic to outlying destinations became increasingly uneconomic. One box of chicks arrived at Farringdon after delivery facilities had been withdrawn; the stationmaster tried to send a telegram asking the consignee to collect only to find that the GPO were no more keen to serve outlying areas and were sending the telegram by taxi. In the end both chicks and telegram shared the vehicle and the two parties the cost!

A lost homing pigeon fared worse when the stationmaster eventually managed to contact its owner. After driving 15 miles to collect the errant bird and paying 5s for the railway services he rang its neck observing, 'If it can't find its way home it's no good to me!'

Swingers

Any horsebox or van attached to the rear of a passenger train to achieve a rapid journey was commonly referred to as a 'swinger', derived from the tendency for such light vehicles to sway alarmingly when last in the train. Goods guards who worked the express freight services experienced this motion regularly.

The fastest freight services were those provided for perishable commodities. These trains were made up of vans fully fitted with vacuum brakes, categorised Class C and timed to run at the fastest possible speeds. The author's one personal journey in the brake van of a Class C express freight train conveying meat traffic from Aberdeen to London will never be forgotten. The dramatic, wildly swaying, madly speeding night-time trip in a small van lit only by an oil lamp was truly memorable, and not a little uncomfortable!

FOUR

ANIMALS AND BIRDS

The link between railways and animals goes right back to the beginnings of railed transport. Horses acted as motive power on the earliest lines while contemporary prints of the Liverpool & Manchester Railway show it carrying sheep in a two-tiered wagon and a carriage horse being transported in better style than the company's third class passengers. Railway use of horses for collection and delivery work and for shunting continued right into the BR era.

Most goods stations had a cattle dock for loading and unloading animals carried by train and strict regulations existed for their care in transit. Livestock consignments varied in size from an elephant to a box of day-old chicks. Some required just a warm spot in a guard's van, others, such as the extensive business in carrying racing pigeons, demanded special trains and a careful, documented release of the birds before their race home.

The Penny Puffer

This was the colloquial name given to the Millwall Extension Railway's services between Millwall Junction in East London and the Thames at North Greenwich. However, at one period it would have been inappropriate, for trains on the section through the docks had to be hauled by horses because of the risk of steam engines setting fire to the host of sails so near the route.

Canine in Control

The day had started quite normally for most of the footplate staff at Worcester, with the minor exception of one driver's small problem. His wife, who normally took care of the family Alsatian, had been called away leaving her husband with no alternative but to take his dog to work with him. His roster involved driving a morning diesel multiple unit train to Oxford and, since there was no one else available to take over the job, the

PETERBOROUGH STATION.

The new railways depended as much on horses as had the stage coach era.
They were needed to work to and from stations as this illustrated *London
News* scene at Peterborough shows.

running foreman reluctantly agreed to the dog accompanying his master
in the Metro Cammell unit's driving cab. He knew it was a well-behaved
animal, so there really should not be a problem. It could lie on the cab floor
and lowering the blinds behind the driver would mean that none of the
passengers would notice the stowaway.

Down the line the day had also started normally for the train's intending
passengers. There were a few at Pershore and quite a few at Evesham,
possibly remembering the time when they had a service between Ashchurch
and Birmingham New Street from the adjacent Midland station. Be that as
it may, their musings came to an abrupt end with the approach of their own
train. As it drew nearer they could hardly believe their eyes. It was being
driven by a dog! An Alsatian was sitting on the driver's seat with its paws on
the control panel and was turning its head to eye its customers as the train
slowly came to a halt!

The driver was later to say, when word of the incident reached 'Authority',
that he had dropped something on the floor of the cab and that his action
in bending down to pick it up caused the dog to stir, rear up and place its
front paws on the driving panel. He expressed himself sorry for what had
happened and no official action was taken, but the legend of the canine
driver soon became firmly established in the folklore of the Cotswold Line.

Cats and Dogs

Cats and dogs have featured as much in railway life as in other walks. Many a station cat earned its keep by catching rodents, but Preston's resident cat had only three legs and relied more on charity than action. It was known as 'Lucky' because it had survived being hit by a freight train.

A better class of cat was often to be found on its way to try for a prize at some exhibition or other. In one case at Glasgow, Buchanan Street, several of them had to be transferred between trains. Their baskets had a label asking for the well-bred animals to be watered en route but, fed up with confinement, they promptly dashed off when the basket doors were opened. After a moment of panic and some energetic but futile chasing, the station staff imaginatively rounded up the local strays and sent them off to London instead. What the judges thought is not recorded!

When Herbert Taylor was stationmaster at Attleborough his dog used to ride about the area by train, completely on its own, and accorded a welcome and titbits wherever it alighted. Several stations had dogs that collected money for charity and some are still remembered by plaques at their home stations; 'Dandy' of Weston-super-Mare was one and 'Station Jim' of Slough another. The latter also went walkabout on occasions but he did collect £40 for the GWR Widows & Orphans Fund before his death in 1896, and is remembered for his 'armoury of tricks'. At weekends 'London Jack', with his mistress Mrs Wickens, collected money from passengers at Waterloo station for the London & South Western Railway Servants' Orphanage.

Horses

Railways may have displaced the long-distance horse-drawn coaches but the link with the horse was to continue for many years. Privately operated horse buses served the new stations while the collection and delivery of goods traffic was entirely dependent on horse-drawn drays. Each major goods station had its horses, carters and stables and many used horses to carry out minor shunting movements in the absence of a train or pilot engine. The Liverpool & Manchester Railway was the first of many that undertook to carry private carriages and their horses. Many a quality horse from Lambourn, Newmarket or one of the other training areas travelled by rail to a show or racecourse. These vehicles had a small compartment for a groom and the horse tackle and were frequently attached to the rear of passenger trains.

As late as 1962 Newmarket received 748 horses during the year and despatched 1,182. Some of the horseboxes used would have been positioned

The shunting horse will start to move his three wagons after the shunter has finished posing, brake stick in hand, for the camera.

by 'Charlie' or 'Butch' who were British Rail's last two working horses. They were in the charge of horse loading foreman Bill Hulyer, who had worked at Newmarket for forty one years, but they knew their job so well that very little direction was needed. The shunting horse at Bletchley even had his own hut in the goods yard!

Not that working with horses was without incident. One in particular involved a pony and trap kept at the old Great Eastern Railway offices at Hamilton House, near Liverpool Street. It was used for visiting the stables at Bishopsgate but on one occasion its user was just getting into the trap when the local horse-drawn fire engine rushed past, sounding its bell with a great clamour. The railway pony pricked up its ears and promptly set off in pursuit with the petrified clerk hanging on for dear life. The runaway did not slow down until it reached Cheapside, the location of the fire. Eventually the bemused railwayman got back to base but then had some difficulty in explaining his lengthy absence, until someone remembered that the pony had previously worked for the fire brigade!

Quite a different aspect of the link between horses and railways is revealed by Section XXXVI of the Caterham Railway Act which stipulated:

That wherever the said Railway shall run parallel with or near any part of the Roads under the jurisdiction of the Trustees of the Surrey and Sussex [turnpike] Roads … there shall be erected … screen walls, earth banks or close fences, so constructed as effectually to prevent horses travelling along such roads from seeing the trains passing along the Railway.

Most horses are good tempered, but not one particular milkman's horse in Worcester where Fred Jones' first railway job was as a 'knocker-up'. It was bad enough that in one road the two men he had to rouse lived at opposite ends of the street, but infinitely worse was the fact that the milkman's horse tried very hard to bite him in between. Until, that is, Fred learned to keep off the pavement by jumping over garden fences.

Donkeys

The 0-4-2T locomotive and trailer set working the GWR's Marlow branch was universally known as *The Marlow Donkey*. Doubtless semi-affectionate, the term was not meant to denote speed, but, on the other hand, the donkey belonging to George Hoy of 7 Chester Street, Bethnal Green, clearly enjoyed a better reputation. Mr Hoy was unhappy about the service from Sudbury to London and in 1856 sent a challenge to the directors of the Eastern Counties Railway to match one of their trains against his donkey and cart. He is reported to have won, but it seems unlikely that even the unloved Eastern Counties Railway would have been bested by a donkey and cart.

Cows

Now, everyone knows that cows are gentle, placid creatures not much given to urgency or speed, except – apparently – those that graze in pastures bordering rural railways. Such cows clearly feel a strong need to secure a place in the legends that surround any remote line of character, especially one that has been built under a Light Railway Order.

The standard legend usually involves someone like a villager returning from market. His train had just restarted after passing over a level crossing and the guard closing the gates behind it, when the brakes went on again and the guard had to go forward to investigate. As he returned past the villager's compartment he obliging volunteered the explanation, 'Cows on the line.' Back in his van the guard gave 'right away' to the driver on the footplate and off the train went again, only to repeat the performance after a couple of hundred yards. 'Another cow on the line?' queried the passenger. 'No,' replied the guard, 'same one; it passed us!'

Much further north a stationmaster on a lonely single line had long been suspected of having too many sidelines for the proper execution of his railway duties. In an attempt to catch him out an 'officers' special' was laid on to pay a visit without any warning. Nearing its destination the special train was held up waiting for someone to release the token for the single line leading to the station under scrutiny, and its occupants began to believe that all their worst fears were well founded. Eventually the release was given, and the special went forward. The stationmaster rushed over to explain his absence with the time-honoured excuse 'Cows on the line, sir'. Not to be put off easily, the officers insisted on inspecting the damage they had done but, as the wily stationmaster had made good use of their delayed arrival to visit a nearby field with a bucket and shovel, several immaculate cow pats between the rails made his story unchallengeable.

Hugh Jenkins used to tell of returning to his home depot at Swindon in a train that ran into a herd of cattle that had strayed onto the main line. He alighted and joined in the clear-up operation, while the train went forward under caution for examination at Swindon where it was found to be badly damaged and had to be taken out of service. The impact area was a mess and clearing it in pouring rain was a miserable job, Hugh having a particularly difficult task in removing the hide of one dead animal from a set of trailing points.

At the time Hugh was lecturing to evening classes at Swindon College and could only get there by going straight from the scene of the mishap. He described his late arrival as 'in a notably dishevelled state, looking like the foreman from the local abattoir and stinking of Bovril'.

Bull Running

The former yearly Bull Running event at Stamford, Lincolnshire, consisted essentially of closing the town gates and harrying a bull around the streets until it dropped. Despite a 1788 proclamation that the activity was unlawful and punishable by death, and the use of dragoons to try to enforce this, the bull run continued for nearly 200 years.

Jim Cherry, a friend of the author's father, used to tell of a later bull which may have sensed some latent local hostility, for it escaped while being unloaded at Stamford East station and promptly set about terrorising the railway staff. After rampaging around the yard for an hour it was finally recaptured, but quickly got away again and plunged into the River Welland in an attempt to swim across. To add insult to injury the exhausted bull was soon in danger of drowning and had to be rescued by those it had been tormenting.

The Circus comes to Town

Railways regularly moved a whole circus – people, animals, equipment and tents, the lot – and became very proficient at doing so. They provided the vital link in the circus programme of visits which could involve as many as 2,000 miles of movement over a season. The key to success was the pre-planning undertaken by the railway operating people and the circus transport officer. The former would schedule the train paths, order the special vans required, roster the staff and issue an operating notice to ensure everyone understood what was to be done. The circus would link performance times with the need to walk animals to the station and provide a 'train master' to marshal the loading of the wheeled vehicles to the 45ft bogie flat wagons using a tractor and the railway end dock.

The circus horses travelled three to a horse box while double-ended vans were used for the ponies, donkeys, camels and llamas. Grooms travelled with the larger animals to keep an eye on their comfort and meet their need for company. Smaller ones had their own travelling cages and all the tentage and other equipment was packed by the circus in their own ingenious way and stowed in covered vans.

At one period the Bertram Mills circus had six elephants who became regular rail travellers. They were provided with long coats for the journey and walked solemnly from the circus field to the station before queuing patiently for their turn to climb the ramp into the covered van provided for their exclusive use. Most would lie down during the journey but, curiously, one always remained standing and on guard. Mostly things went smoothly, but loading a young, inexperienced Chipperfield elephant once caused a few dramatic moments. He wanted to join the others in the van but was nervous of the loading ramp, despite the transverse slats fitted to ensure an animal's feet had a good grip. Pushing gently but encouragingly from behind seemed to be the answer and several station staff joined in the effort. Unfortunately, the tension of the occasion caused the elephant to pass a stream of water which sprayed back off the slats and drenched everyone in the vicinity. He then stood there, halfway up the ramp, seemingly well pleased with the array of astonished, bedraggled and dripping 'helpers' his action had created.

Droving

Until the motor vehicle took over animals were moved between stations and markets on the hoof. The racehorses unloaded at Bishops Cleeve and walked the two miles to Cheltenham Racecourse quietly enough, but driving geese to market from Norwich Victoria station was always a noisy and unruly affair. The Great Western had its own field at Carmarthen for holding cattle but escapees from the subsequent drive to market occasionally paid an unwelcome call at the cottages en route. One bull, bent on being

Clifton Down Station yard on a Sunday afternoon after the end of a Royal Show.
Locomotive No.2927 *St Patrick* is at the head of a train of horseboxes and cattle wagons.

different, headed off along the permanent way until he was recaptured by
the signalman at Abergwili Junction.

Farms and Shows

Royal and county shows were big business for the railways, requiring
extensive planning to ensure traffic arrived on time and that enough delivery
vehicles and cranes were provided to get the marquees and stands onto the
showground in the right order and condition. Since only top-class animals
were exhibited great care had to be taken over their journey arrangements.

Before the last war any farmer moving to another farm usually did so by
rail. An example in 1937 involved a journey from Towcester to Newark and
the rail carriage of some 500 animals, four containers of household goods
and 20 tons of farm implements. Since there were 100 milking cows among
the animal contingent the special train journey had to be timed to depart
after milking on one day and before milking on the next.

FIVE

BEST-LAID PLANS

The railway industry is a highly organised and well-planned activity. The timetables are a complex reconciliation of passenger needs, line capacity, rolling stock availability and the rostering of railwaymen. Providing the track and signalling is equally complex and there are dozens of ancillary functions to be arranged, such as design, maintenance, publicity and catering.

Despite all the planning, in an age when popular television features a variety of programmes devoted to the gaffes, mishaps and inadvertencies of show business, it is hardly surprising to find that similar situations occur in other walks of life, even in the railway industry. Safety is sacrosanct but humour and oddity abound.

Best-laid plans do not always work out and good intentions are not always enough.

Matthew ch.7 v.24

One hundred and fifty years to the day after the opening of the pioneer Canterbury & Whitstable Railway the Invicta 150 programme of anniversary celebrations included a civic procession to Canterbury Cathedral for a service and then a luncheon for invited guests in a marquee in nearby Westgate Gardens. It had rained the night before but the weather was kind on 3 May 1980 itself and all went exceedingly well, until the various groups of hungry people approached the immaculate tables prepared for their satisfaction. With hindsight the Archbishop might appropriately have referred to Matthew's Gospel chapter seven and its allusion to a house built on sand for, as the guests sat down, the slim metal legs of their chairs sank into turf still soggy from the earlier rain and canted at every conceivable angle. Composure and dignity promptly suffered an hilarious reverse but the meal proved excellent and good humour soon returned. Perhaps this was a reminder that the promoters of the original railway had, despite better advice, chosen a route which also involved boggy ground and had then experienced similar consequences.

'Bumper' Harris

The now familiar escalator seems to have originated with the famous 'sliding staircase' which was incorporated in the Crystal Palace in 1899 and for which a fare of one penny was charged. The Liverpool Overhead Railway installed a similar device at its Seaforth station in 1901 and an escalator also featured at the Earls Court Exhibition in the 1911 Coronation year. On that occasion the fare was only a ha'penny.

The first escalator serving a London tube station was one opened at Earls Court station on 4 October 1911 to link the Piccadilly and District lines. Travellers were doubtful about this new-fangled contraption and to boost confidence in it one 'Bumper' Harris, a man with a wooden leg, was employed to travel up and down all day long. It was felt that seeing him use the escalator would reassure the nervous. Apparently he lost his job when a woman was overheard telling her small son, 'Now you see what happens to people who use these fancy inventions.'

Our Light Railway

This is the title of a sixty-two-line poem in the Somerset dialect which began:

> There ez a line in Zummerzet,
> (And Aw! To think o't makes I zwet):

The WC&P locomotive *Hesperus* in trouble in 1934 when the bridge leading to the company's coal jetty collapsed underneath her.

The queerest, quaintest thing I ween
That ivver wuz by martal zeen.

It appeared in the *Weston-super-Mare Gazette* in 1925 and the object of its
affectionate rhyming was the Weston, Clevedon & Portishead (WC&P)
Railway, a local railway of great character which was eventually to become
part of the Colonel Stephens 'stable' of such lines.

During its forty plus years of operation the WC&P gave rise to many of
the type of apocryphal stories that attached themselves to the smaller and less
formal railways. It was alleged that the cow-catchers on its American-style
passenger saloons always faced to the rear, that train staff regularly stopped
to pick mushrooms or blackberries and that they would quite readily reverse
their train for a missed stop or tardy passenger. One impatient traveller who
asked the driver whether he could go faster was told, 'Yes, sir, but I'm not
supposed to leave the engine!'

The special and unusual character of the Weston, Clevedon & Portishead
Railway seemed, somehow, to survive its wartime closure. Proposals to
reopen the line, for example, foundered because the company seal and shares
had been lost. Even when, forty years on, Christopher Redwood produced
his excellent book on the line, the unconventional spirit of the quaint old
railway still seemed to be around.

Part of the launch publicity for the Redwood book involved its author
being interviewed by Roger Bennett of the local BBC Points West radio
programme. Likeable, able and professional, Roger felt that the interview
would be more atmospheric if he recorded it at a point on the old trackbed
about halfway between Weston and Clevedon and where the route had
crossed the River Yeo. It was to begin with Christopher singing a little ditty
associated with the line.

We should have been warned by our considerable difficulty in finding and
reaching the appointed spot and by the attempts of a pair of over-inquisitive
cows to nudge the singing author down the muddy bank and into the river.
Then the heavens opened and Roger's list of carefully prepared questions
turned into streaky black lines on his clipboard. Attempts to recover either
footing or the process of coherent question and answer proved quite
impossible and uncontrollable laughter finally triumphed. Perhaps it was
no coincidence that all this took place on almost the exact spot where the
WC&P locomotive *Hesperus* fell into a rhine in April 1934!

An Invitation to
the launch of

'THE COTSWOLD & MALVERN EXPRESS'

on

Monday 14 May 1984

* * * * * * *

We look forward to seeing you.
Please bring this invitation with you.

Invitation to the launch of *The Cotswold & Malvern Express.*

The Goat's Story

'It's so long ago now that no one will get upset if I tell the other side of the notorious *Cotswold & Malvern Express* business. You see I was one of the two goats involved in that affair on Monday 14 May 1984 and with so much notoriety resulting from what happened on that day it's high time our version of the events was related.

'The occasion was BR's public launch of a new High Speed Train service from Paddington and the local management had decided to make an event of it by putting aside a couple of coaches on the train for invited guests and showing them something of what the Cotswolds and the Malverns had to offer. In conjunction with the Heart of England Tourist Board there was to be a joint civic reception and buffet lunch on arrival at Worcester and then a coach tour around the beauty spots in the Malvern Hills. On the journey to Worcester the guests were to be cared for by staff dressed in period costume, reflecting the area's links with the Royalist traditions of the Civil War. They would be given travel and tourist information and plied with refreshments which, incidentally, included a locally made and pretty strong cider. Then, at the last minute (as usual) some bright spark came up with the idea of parading animals from the Cotswold Farm Park on the train to represent another of the many tourist attractions of the area through which it was to travel.

'As a result of all this, a fellow goat and I had been roused early from our comfortable pen in the park and told we had to give yet another dreary public performance. Told, you notice, not asked! Still, it was a change from routine, even flattering in a way, but in the excitement of getting ready I failed to breakfast properly, something I was later to regret.

'The train, I must say, was pretty impressive and the VIPs were clearly already having a good time when we joined it. My friend and I both tried to match the festive mood and were quite touched that a nice red carpet had been laid the length of the coaches for our toilet use although, curiously,

On board
the inaugural
*Cotswold &
Malvern Express*
– before the
incident with
the goats.

some excitement seemed to break out when we had taken advantage of it. What I did think was thoughtless, though, was the habit of continually moving the trays of snacks every time we tried to take our turn at eating and before long I began to feel quite faint with hunger. Now, I swear I thought that no one would notice or mind if I made do with the colourful skirt of one of the young ladies in special costume but, when I had chewed no more than halfway up its length, she turned round and made the most almighty fuss, trying to back away, screaming and generally doing the drama queen bit. Consternation and confusion followed and, before we knew it, we'd been hustled away, locked in some hostile van area and then chucked off the train. We were devastated. Just think how you would have felt if it had been you!

'I did hear that the rest of the event went reasonably well for the organisers, although the cider had its effect on a few of the guests who missed the return working back to London. Not that we got any of the special brew; nor any thanks come to that.'

The Stirrup Cup

By the late 1960s the Freightliner network was well established but did not provide a complete national coverage. Southampton had a terminal at Millbrook, South Wales had two – at Cardiff Pengam and Swansea Dan-y-Graig – but Bristol and the south-west peninsular could only be served by unacceptably long collection and delivery movements by road. After a lot of planning and the examination of several possible sites it was decided to set up 'mini terminals' at Bristol, Plymouth and Par to remedy this gap in the

One of the mini Freightliner terminals established in the south-west, in this case the one set up alongside Par station in 1968.

network. These would function in the same way as the larger terminals, but take up much less space as the transfer of containers between wagons and road vehicles would be by mobile crane instead of the more conventional fixed overhead cranes and the 'train' portions would be smaller.

At Plymouth the site selected was at Friary, the former Southern Railway station which had lost its passenger services in 1958 but remained in use as a goods depot. To provide some publicity for the new venture the PR people planned a small ceremony around the departure of the first service from the yard and invited a select group of guests chosen from trade and industry and from the media.

It being the colder time of year the provision of a punch bowl and a home-devised punch was calculated both to warm the press representatives and to engender feelings of goodwill towards the venture. There would be a 'photo opportunity' in which the west of England divisional manager toasted the event with a glass of the punch and waved a guard's flag to speed the first train on its journey.

All would have been well if the press representatives had arrived at the same time, but they came singly and the toasting and flag waiving had to be repeated to satisfy the picture requirements of each new arrival. Inevitably this had its effect on the principal actor in the drama whose flag waving could only be described as highly erratic by the time the last performance had finally taken place. The supporting cast watched the deterioration with great anxiety but fortunately none of the pressmen noticed and all the coverage was gratifyingly objective.

The One-Ship Dock

In an attempt to relieve the Great Eastern Railway of some of its King's Lynn Docks traffic, the Great Northern Railway in 1875 bought a majority interest in a scheme to build a dock at Sutton Bridge, to which the GN had gained access in 1866 over the Peterborough, Wisbech & Sutton Bridge Railway. The new dock opened on 14 May 1881 and celebrated the arrival of its first ship which unloaded a cargo of Norwegian timber. When it left with coal the following day it was clear that the entrance lock was not watertight and a consulting engineer had to be called in. His report proved very bad news and revealed that the sandy soil of the dock base was quite unstable. Even worse, he advised strongly against rebuilding and the venture had to be abandoned.

Anger Management

At one period the London Division of BR(W) ran a series of weekend 'preview' trains to West Country resorts. Cheap fares were offered and the resorts collaborated in providing facilities for the passengers in an effort to encourage them to take summer holidays there. One such train was planned to include a stop at Teignmouth where the hoteliers and local council gladly agreed to arrange a special welcome. Their representatives were at the station on the fateful day but, to their great consternation, saw the train rush through without stopping. The terrible BR 'failure' got headlines in the local papers and a fair amount of unflattering coverage in the nationals.

Leslie Bracey, the West of England Division's commercial manager, shot down to Teignmouth to face the wrath of those who had put a lot of time and money into their part of the venture. Leslie was an able, likeable man, never short of a novel view or the words to express it. He managed to convince the resort interests that the publicity they had received was of such immense value that the driver's failure to stop was really little short of a godsend!

Automania

In the 1980s, when the people at the British Railways Board headquarters – known informally and universally as 'The Kremlin' – were intent on securing economies wherever they could, the divisional manager at Birmingham was due for the replacement of his staff car. He not only put forward the idea that divisional managers should have a car manufactured in their own division but suggested that it would be unwise, and possibly affect freight revenue, if he visited the Rover works in anything less than a top-of-the-range Rover. The arguments worked and, in due course, he got one. Thinking to ride the same bandwagon Hugh Jenkins at Stoke rather fancied a Bentley Mulsanne Turbo and was about to put this idea forward when someone pointed out that Tamworth, also in the Stoke Division, was the home of the Reliant Robin.

Misplaced Optimism

Paddington station was re-signalled in the mid-1960s, a huge task involving the work of many signal boxes being concentrated in a new panel box at Old Oak Common. In addition, Paddington's old wooden island platforms were rebuilt, the approach track layout improved and the London Transport lines separated from those of BR now that a connection was no longer required for running freight trains through to Smithfield Market depot. Meticulous planning was followed by five weeks of civil engineering work which necessitated closing first one half of the station and then the other and diverting trains to Kensington Olympia, Ealing Broadway and Marylebone.

The whole operation – publicity, train alterations and engineering work – went like clockwork and compliments far exceeded complaints. Thus encouraged, the publicity department, to mark the successful completion of the work, prepared some enormous posters saying 'BACK TO NORMAL. THANKS FOR YOUR CO-OPERATION'. No sooner had these appeared than the whole service collapsed into a shambles as staff struggled to come to terms with their new station and its new technology!

Ingratitude

The introduction of High Speed Trains on the Western Region was quite a revolution in terms of both service and operation. The first trial run to Cardiff was so important that the BRB chairman himself, Peter Parker at the time, travelled on the train. Just before the return journey it was found that two female Canadian visitors had missed their train to London and, in the interests of good public relations, the chairman was asked if he would 'give them a lift' on the trial special. He agreed and their problem was solved.

Now this would all have made a nice little press story but when reporters, seeking the views of these impromptu passengers on their experience, asked for their reactions to travelling at 125mph it all went pear shaped. 'Oh dear,' said one of the two, 'we'd never have travelled on it if we'd known it was going to go at that speed!'

SIX

UNUSUAL SYSTEMS

Two major influences on railway transport were the search for the best technical and mechanical methods in the earlier years, and the search for economy and profits in those that followed. The former resulted in quite a few unusual ideas being tried in the traction and equipment fields and the latter in the provision of some rather curious facilities.

Applying these factors to differing terrains and adding that peculiar nineteenth-century dimension that produced so many inventive engineers led to atmospheric railways, monorails, rack railways, water balance inclines and a host of other peculiar variants.

Sail Railways

There are references to a 'Wind-way' and to 'Sailing Waggons' operating in south Wales before the end of the eighteenth century and to proposals to use wind power on two lines built on Henry Palmer's monorail principle in 1824–25. More specifically, a sail-car was certainly used on Britain's first pier railway at Herne Bay in 1833. The pier's backer was Sir Henry Oxendon who had already experimented with land and ice yachts and now extended his novel thinking to a rail yacht. This took the form of a single passenger vehicle, grandly named *Old Neptune's Car*, and fitted with a lug sail that could replace the normal manual propulsion when the wind was favourable. Another Kent sail-rail location was at Cliffe where a two-masted sailing trolley seems to have been used on one of the industrial tramways of that area.

For several years, from around 1837, wind power was used on the Newtyle & Coupar Angus Railway according to a later report in the *Dundee Weekly News*. Apparently, when the wind was favourable a tarpaulin was fixed to the end of a passenger carriage to form a crude sail. However, since the horse still had to follow behind in case of a mishap or a drop in the breeze the potential gain seems minimal.

The track of the Snowdon Mountain Railway that uses the rack system and steam locomotives with inclined boilers for its five-mile climb up the mountain.

A former seaman turned grocer living in Middlesbrough in the 1840s is said to have used the same approach on the straight section of the Stockton & Darlington line to South Stockton. To get to the Quaker Meeting House on Sunday when the line was otherwise closed to traffic he would use an old carriage fitted with mast and sail which could be used instead of the horse when the wind was right. Using a lug sail would have permitted catching wind from most quarters but, clearly, any mast-supporting carriage could only operate on a route devoid of overbridges. This 8-mile round trip may well have been a record for sail railway operation.

Another century brought another example of sail traction. This was on the 3.5-mile standard gauge line built for the War Department from Kilnsea along a narrow strip of land jutting out into the sea on the north side of the Humber estuary. It originated during the First World War to permit access to the lighthouse, lifeboat and signal station at Spurn Point and to carry materials for the construction of Bull Fort to guard the vital Humber harbours. It was also used to bring in materials for strengthening the sea defences. The contractors used five steam locomotives to haul works trains during the construction period.

Although a small locomotive and single carriage were used on the line the majority of the official journeys were carried out by, at first, a motor trolley and then by small railcars. However, the Spurn Head Railway does seem to have been run informally enough for the local fishing, lifeboat and coastguard community to devise their own private movements on it using a conventional flat four-wheeled trolley fitted with a lug sail. The trolley also had a longitudinal plank extending 'fore and aft', on which the driver sat with his arm extending out to monitor the boom on one side of the contraption while his passengers sat sideways on the other to counterbalance the weight of the sail. Braking was primitive and both runaways and accidents occurred!

Before the railway closed in the 1950s it had also been used by a converted pre-1914 racing car fitted with flanged wheels.

'Dead Meat Trains'

For eighty-seven years the Southern Railway and its London & South Western (L&SW) Railway predecessor moved train loads of coffins from Waterloo to the Brookwood cemetery of the London Necropolis & National Mausoleum Co. For many years two trains ran every day from the company's private station adjacent to the London main line terminus and made the 28-mile journey to Brookwood and the private siding which then led to the two stations in the huge cemetery. From 1928 the service was reduced to two trains a week and finally ended in 1941 as a result of the Luftwaffe bombing of London.

This unusual activity, rather insensitively nicknamed by railwaymen, had its origins in a London cholera epidemic in 1848–49 which killed around 15,000 people and brought the chronic overcrowding in London graveyards to crisis point. By an Act of 1852 the London Necropolis Co. was authorised to 'establish and maintain a cemetery in the Parish of Woking' and to 'contract with the L&SW for the carrying of bodies in properly constructed carriages to the cemetery from either Waterloo or Nine Elms stations'. Attended by proper ceremony and solemnity, the service began two years later. The company not only used special trains but had hearses to collect the coffins, steam-powered lifts to raise them to the platform mortuaries and station waiting rooms for each class of attendant passenger. Special return fares were offered for up to six mourners with each coffin, the occupants being carried for 2s 6d in the case of paupers, 5s for working men and 20s for the well-to-do. On the train the latter were carried in their own highly ornate compartment.

The 2,000-acre Brookwood site purchased from Lord Onslow was to become the world's largest burial ground when opened. Business was so brisk that the Necropolis Co. sought and paid for the building of the main line station at Brookwood. However, as cremation became commonplace over the years, the demand for the 'dead meat trains' declined and the final bombing merely hastened their inevitable demise.

The Never-Stop Railway

Something like 26 million people visited the 1924 British Empire Exhibition at Wembley Park, a large proportion of them arriving via Wembley Park (Met), Wembley Hill (LNER-GC) or the special stadium loop from the Marylebone line.

Within the site a double track, 2ft 8in gauge, railway was constructed with five stations along its 6,600ft length to serve various parts of the exhibition. Passengers were conveyed in 20ft long single cars propelled by the use of a revolving shaft housed in a concrete trough below rail level and which, in effect, screwed the cars along. They ran in close formation with a shorter shaft pitch at the stations slowing the vehicles down to about 1.5mph and loops enabling them to reverse direction at each end of the line. The system needed no staff.

Pneumatic Propulsion

To publicise the potential of pneumatic propulsion an underground demonstration line was designed by the Victorian engineer T.W. Rammell and built in 1864 to carry visitors to and from the Crystal Palace. The system consisted of a single carriage with glass end doors running in a 600-yard-long, curved tunnel and fitted with an airtight bristle collar. From the upper terminus the carriage descended by gravity into the tunnel where air-tight doors closed behind it and air pressure, generated by a steam engine in the

Brunel tried the atmospheric system on the South Devon Railway's line through Dawlish but the pipes could not be kept airtight.

fan house, completed the movement. A return fare of sixpence was charged for the short journey.

Although work was begun on another such line by the Waterloo & Whitehall Railway this was not completed. Nor did the Crystal Palace venture last very long before falling into disuse.

Wild Cars

Mines and quarries had a reputation for applying ingenuity to challenges but no result could have been more hair-raising than the 'Ceir Gwylltion', or 'Wild Cars', used in the Craig Ddu Quarry near Blaenau Ffestiniog. The three main inclines of the quarry consisted of about a mile of double-track 2ft gauge line rising at 1 in 6 to a height of about 1,000ft. There were plenty of empty wagons going up the inclines and able to get the quarrymen to work but no spare descending capacity to help them get back to the Blaenau road after the end of their shift.

Some very basic domestic engineering soon provided each man with his own simple car which was operated by gravity on the two inner rails of the twin tracks so as to improve stability and stay clear of the winding cable and its rollers which ran between each normal pair of rails. Each car was just a simple board above one track with an outrigger to the other. The board held the rail by using a small wheel beneath the front and a skid at the rear. Sitting on this board with a simple friction brake between his knees the rider launched himself downward and relied on his judgement, and that of everyone else plunging down behind, to achieve a safe descent!

The quarrymen's cars on the Padarn Railway were officially called Velocipedes but the men referred to these, too, as 'Wild Cars'. They were a cut above the Craig Ddu examples, having a four-wheel chassis and seating for sixteen. Owned co-operatively by groups of workers, one type was operated by hand and the other by foot treadle. Racing, speeding and accidents were not unknown but, here again, the users were practical men, skilled with machinery and in their home environment, and the wild cars fulfilled a very useful role until superseded by more conventional workmen's trains in 1895.

GBR – George Bennie Railplane

After the end of the First World War a surplus of redundant airship and aircraft engines led to schemes in Germany for using these to propel railway vehicles. Initial developments were confined to normal rail vehicles and a shunting engine so powered was operated in Berlin around 1920. Ten years later a 28-ton passenger coach fitted with a 600hp engine driving a propeller achieved a speed of 140mph on conventional rail track.

These ideas and the successful monorail system at Wuppertal led inventor George Bennie to show a model of his so-called 'railplane' to the Royal Assocation in 1928. The design consisted of a light, streamlined coach with a propeller at each end and suspended in true monorail fashion. In the remarkably short time of two years a 426ft test track had been erected over an LNER line at Milngavie, Glasgow.

First operated on 3 July 1930, the Bennie line, as installed at Milngavie, consisted of a lattice box girder supporting the main rail which carried the two-wheel suspension bogies at each end of the one car actually built. Horizontal rubber-tyred stability wheels ran on lighter girders beneath, one for each direction of travel. Gripper brakes acted on the longitudinal girders and the whole structure was mounted on steel trestles 80ft apart, and could be varied in height to accommodate gradients. The shafts for the four-blade propellers also formed the car couplings.

The GBR system was also considered for routes to Manchester, in Cornwall, from Waltham Abbey to Dagenham and for linking London and Paris but no backers were forthcoming and the original track just rusted away until claimed for scrap by war needs.

Opened in 1890 the 900ft Lynton & Lynmouth Cliff Railway provides an important link between Lynmouth at the mouth of the West Lyn River and Lynton high above.

Cliff Railways

Most of Britain's numerous cliff railways were designed to improve the link between beach and cliffs at popular holiday resorts. Some installations were powered by a stationary engine, but quite a few of the two-car lines employed the water balance method where the cars were linked by a cable running around a drum at the upper station, and a tank below the descending one was filled with sufficient water to make it heavier than its mate. The water was then drained off at the lower station after the descent. Quite a few of these short, steeply inclined lines are still in use.

A Railway with Lifebelts

Unlikely as it may seem Britain once had a railed system equipped with lifebelts and a lifeboat! This was the Brighton & Rottingdean Seashore Electric Tramway, a 2.75-mile beach tramway using cars elevated on legs so that operation could continue even when tides swept over the shoreline route up to a depth of 15ft. There were two tracks of 2ft 8.5in gauge with the vehicle legs resting on two four-wheeled bogies, powered by four 25hp electric motors which collected their current trolley-style from a trackside supply. The 50ft long cars could carry 150 people.

This odd-looking system was wrecked in a freak storm a few weeks after its opening in November 1896. It was back at work by August 1897 but succumbed to the need for groin lengthening on the foreshore in 1902.

Island Monorail

The beginnings of residential development on Canvey Island included plans for a tramway from the Benfleet ferry crossing to Leigh Beck on the south-east corner of the island. To provide access for potential buyers while it was being built the promoter, Frederick Hester, operated what he called a Mono-Metal Tramway over the route from 1901 to 1904. This was a horse-worked monorail using a single low-slung wooden car with passengers seated longitudinally and the horse harnessed in a parallel frame. There was a small seat projecting forward for the driver who held the horse's reins and operated a simple brake.

Work had just started on the tramway and its power station when an exceptionally high spring tide in 1904 flooded the works and brought both construction and residential interest to an end.

Inclines

Rope-worked inclines were commonplace in the early days of railways but as locomotives became more powerful they were later confined to industrial lines, especially in areas like County Durham where dozens were used to move coal down to staithes on the Tyne and Wear, to Seaham Harbour or to the main line network.

Many were still in use in the 1960s but twenty years later the only commercial operation was on the NCB's railway from South Hetton Colliery to Seaham Harbour. There, rakes of six wagons of colliery waste were still being lowered to the harbour by the traditional counter-balance method in which the weight of the descending loads help to haul empties back up the incline. The trackwork at South Hetton included a section with a common centre rail.

The Edge Hill Light Railway was opened in 1920 to bring ironstone down from the top of Edge Hill in Warwickshire to Burton Dassett on the Stratford-upon-Avon & Midland Junction Railway. Single track below and above the incline, this was a half mile section of 1 in 9 on which the initial single track was followed by a double-track loop and then by a three-rail upper part where the central rail was common to both ascending and descending traffic. Wagons were cable-worked on the incline and locomotive-hauled above and below. The line lasted only five years before closing and abandoning a steam excavator and a Manning Wardle LB&SC Terrier 0-4-0ST at the top!

An incline connects colliery and railway in the North Somerset coalfield.

SEVEN

UNUSUAL OPERATION

The experiments of the early railway pioneers, coupled with unusual physical and traffic circumstances and a measure of human vanity and idiosyncrasy, all combined to produce examples of unusual railway working. These diminished as locomotives became more powerful and the skills of civil, mechanical and other engineers found tidier solutions to their problems but the out-of the-ordinary did not entirely disappear. It might have forsaken the main lines but novel and unusual practices survived on many industrial railways and lines in remote locations. Some even became legitimate!

The Canterbury & Whitstable Whim

Opened on 3 May 1830, four months before the great Liverpool & Manchester enterprise, the modest 6-mile railway between Canterbury and Whitstable set a precedent for several of the mistakes to which early railways were to prove prone.

The intention was to link Canterbury with the sea and a route to achieve this was surveyed by John Dixon, one of George Stephenson's associates. He found and recommended a nice, easily graded route but had his ideas rejected by the proprietors who fancied, of all things, a tunnel. They would have cause to rue this apparent whim!

As authorised in 1825 the new railway was to pass over Tyler Hill, and this involved both a tunnel nearly half a mile long and some steep gradients. When completed the line climbed at 1 in 41–56 for the first 1.6 miles out of Canterbury to reach the top of the hill and then needed an even steeper descent of 1 in 28–31 down the other side. Next came an unwelcome patch of boggy ground before the final drop at 1 in 57 into Whitstable. Stationary winding engines had to be installed at either end of the hilltop plateau and train guards were given the job of attaching and detaching the ropes as each section of the journey was completed. Another engine had to be installed when the Stephenson-built locomotive *Invicta* proved adequate only for the

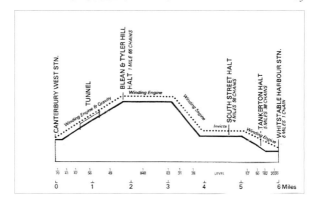

Gradients and haulage arrangements on the Canterbury & Whitstable Railway.

1-mile level stretch north of Bogshole, no wonder the 6-mile journey took an hour to complete, even more when something went wrong and horses had to be used or a large train split into sections.

The failure to heed John Dixon's advice pushed the C&W capital requirements up from the original £31,000 to an eventual £111,000, upon which no dividend was ever paid. Little wonder, too, that the original shares fell in value to only 10s. When the South Eastern Railway took over in 1846 it found that the infamous tunnel had been built in sections of different profile and only old, altered or cut-down stock could work through it. The Canterbury & Whitstable line did bring cheaper coal to Canterbury and, over the years, transported millions of Whitstable Oysters, but it could not sustain passenger trains beyond 1930 nor freight after 1952.

Mixed Gauge Trains

There are several examples of trains consisting of both broad and narrow-gauge stock operating on the GWR before the final demise of the broad-gauge in 1892. They were, of course, confined to mixed-gauge sections of track and a special match wagon had to be used to link the portions together. This truck, which was broad-gauge, was fitted with a coupling chain which slid on a transverse bar at each end. This peculiar arrangement seems to have worked well enough although great care had to be taken when passing over points.

Mixed-gauge passenger trains were at work between Slough and Windsor as early as the 1860s and two regular mixed-gauge goods services were

SOUTHWOLD RAILWAY TRAIN.
SEP 1879 - APRIL 1929.

Mixed trains were
a common feature
of light railway
operation. Many
minor lines, like
the Southwold
Railway pictured
here, just did not
have sufficient
traffic to support
separate passenger
and freight services.

introduced in 1871, one over the Canal Basin branch at Exeter and the other
between Truro and Penzance.

The 1886 timetable records a footnote against train No.121, the 5.15 a.m.
Bridgwater–Taunton goods, stating that 'The engine working this Train is
N.G. with dummy buffers, and will work any Broad Gauge Locomotive
Coal Traffic from Bridgwater to Taunton when required'. The coal it carried
would have been brought by sailing vessel into Bridgwater Docks from south
Wales or the Forest of Dean, but this was the year in which the Severn Tunnel
was opened and affected much of the cross-Channel coal traffic movement.

Mixed Traffic Trains

By the time the Big Four railway companies – the LNER, LMS, GWR and
SR – reached the end of a twenty-five-year existence their few remaining
train services conveying both passenger and goods vehicles were well
regulated. The LNER, for example, broadly limited them to thirty vehicles,
35mph and 10 miles without stopping. Unfitted wagons had to be at the
rear, the engine and coaches had to have continuous braking and a brake van
ratio was stipulated. These basic regulations were varied slightly for special
cases such as circus trains.

In earlier years mixed train operation tended to be rather more informal,
especially on the Highland Railway whose lines were remote from
authority and bedevilled by low traffic levels. Continuous braking on the
passenger portion of such trains had been ordered in 1891 under the 1889
Regulation of Railways Act but the Highland company were still not
complying six years later. This was revealed in a report on an accident on

the Skye branch when a wagon coupling broke as a mixed train climbed to Achterneed and the rear ten vehicles, six of them passenger carriages, ran back for nearly six miles. The occupants were unscathed physically but would probably never forget the experience!

10mph Engine Change

Changing engines on a train meant bringing it to a halt and then several minutes of delay while one engine moved off and its replacement was coupled up. From time to time some thought was given to effecting such a change without stopping.

A 1930 account records such an engine change effected without the 'train' stopping.

It happened on the South Shields, Marsden & Whitburn Colliery Railway and involved an electric locomotive taking over from a steam one. First, the electric locomotive set off ahead of the steam-hauled train and then, when both were on the move but well separated, the steam engine was uncoupled and sprinted ahead. Slick points work diverted it into a siding and reset the route before the now engineless train arrived. The loitering electric locomotive then slowed sufficiently for the train to catch it up and be recoupled. Dramatic, yes, but unlikely to get the approval of the inspecting officer of railways.

Zig-Zags

Although Britain's contours did not require the dramatic railway zig-zags that occur in more mountainous countries there have been a few such layouts on minor and industrial lines, including one at Aberglaslyn on the Welsh Highland Railway and another linking the Taff Bargoed Joint line with Dowlais steelworks in South Wales.

Our most notable example was the Skinningrove Zig-Zag which linked the iron ore mines at Loftus, with the main line along the coast from Whitby to Saltburn. Replacing an earlier 1 in 6 incline it lifted trains 150ft from the mines to the viaduct above by means of two reversing necks and a 1 in 28 centre section. There were occasional mishaps including one potential disaster in which a Whitby train forsook the main line for a brief, unplanned excursion down the 1 in 74 start of the first leg of the zig-zag. Also remarkable is the 1911–13 civil engineering feat that replaced the original viaduct by burying it in 720,000 tons of spoil displaced from the very mines which had weakened its foundations.

At Whitby Prospect Hill an LNER A8 Class 4-6-2T heads a train southbound towards Scarborough. The line from Whitby station is on the left.

Token Dip

The use of tokens to authorise passage over a single line of railway has long been a standard method of ensuring safety. On many routes, such as those of the Midland & Great Northern, token exchange apparatus was fitted to the locomotives to enable the token for one section to be exchanged for that of the next without halting the train. Mostly things went smoothly.

If a token that should have been surrendered was carried through there would be serious delays while it was returned, but one situation was even worse: when a token was lost. This happened quite a few times on the route east from Bedford St Johns towards Sandy where the line follows the River Ouse. The writer has more than once watched a fireman groping in shallow waters to find a token that had not been collected to plan.

Bob Poynter recalls a similar case on the Taunton–Barnstaple branch, involving a Taunton crew who had taken over the engine of a summer Saturday through express from Wolverhampton to Ilfracombe. The locomotive had been steaming badly ever since they left Taunton on the outward run and by the time they left Dulverton on the return was proving a real challenge for the fireman. Working desperately on the fire as they approached Morebath Junction he forgot to set the token catching machine but did manage to grab the token manually. Rather than carry the old one through he gently lobbed it towards the signalman, only to see it disappear into the waters of an adjacent stream.

Crossing the Line

In addition to the level crossings operated from a signal box there were hundreds of others in more remote locations and operated by a crossing keeper. Many of these were women, often the wives of railway employees glad to have an extra income and be able to rent the crossing house or cottage. The basic arrangements provided them with details of the planned train services and advance notice of specials, and placed them on the inter-signal box circuits so that they knew when to open and close gates and to operate any signals they had.

The Norwich district had problems in securing staff for the crossing keeper jobs and even employed a Polish countess at one location. At another, on the March–Wisbech line, there was a lady with an impressive vocabulary, most of which she used when a ballast cleaning train shot the dirty ballast through the windows of her cottage.

One West Country branch line had no Sunday service except for the occasional special during the summer months. Permanent way staff often did maintenance work on Sundays and were glad of the time and three-quarters pay it brought them. One member of the permanent way gang also spent time in dalliance with a local lady crossing keeper until the day when a special surprised them at the height of their passion. Not having seen the special train notice she had not lowered her distant signal or closed the gates. The footplate crew had expected the signal to be off and pressed on without checking. Result: a resounding crash and a new dimension to the phrase 'Has the earth moved for you?'

High Dyke Ore

Authorised in a Great Northern Railway Act of 1912 but not opened until after the First World War, the modest High Dyke mineral branch was to prove a very profitable piece of railway. The 7-mile single line ran west from High Dyke exchange sidings, located on the Down side of the East Coast Main Line just north of Stoke Tunnel, first to Stainby and then on to Sproxton. Some public goods traffic was dealt with but the main activity was the forwarding of ironstone in tippler wagons from the various mines to the steelworks furnaces. Local workings were in the hands of Grantham engines, all fitted with ex-M&GN Whitaker tablet/token exchange apparatus.

The branch was steeply graded, especially near High Dyke and at Colsterworth where the mine area north of the railway had been joined by a second mine south of the branch early in the Second World War. Each

Iron ore excavation at Colsterworth, Lincolnshire, in 1965.

had five holding sidings which were linked to the BR branch by a junction trailing towards High Dyke. The links between the mines and BR were not only at the bottom of a steep dip but were also used by mine locomotives transferring wagons between the two locations.

Arriving on a Brush diesel at the head of a train of empty wagons in 1965 the author was treated to the spectacle of the train being held on the approach descent by the guard's brake while the train engine was detached and admitted to the North sidings.

With the points reset for the 'main' line the wagons were allowed to complete the descent and then held again on the rising gradient beyond. Next the locomotive moved out of the siding and back up the slope, there to be reunited with its train when it was released and allowed by gravity to retrace its original course ready to be propelled onto the mine sidings.

The procedure for outwards traffic was equally unusual. A train of loaded wagons, locomotive leading, would pull out of the sidings and set off eastwards up the slope towards High Dyke. Once clear of the points the Colsterworth signalman would reset the points and the train would reverse up the western slope as if it were to be propelled to Skillington Road. However, this was only a device to give it a good, gravity-aided run at the summit it had to breast before reaching the the the main line.

More Gravity

Dealing with the mass movement of public school pupils and their luggage at the beginning and end of each term called for an unusual amount of planning, organisation and effort. Not so far from High Dyke both Oundle and Uppingham stations were hectic places at such times. Uppingham was also unusual in that the branch line owed its existence to an agreement between the school and the LNWR that the pupils should all travel by rail. School specials were operated even before the public train services began on 1 October 1894.

At one period the short Uppingham branch also provided an example of the use of gravity to run round passenger trains. A set arriving at the Seaton end would be reversed out of the platform after its passengers had alighted and then held on the brake while the locomotive came off and shunted to another line. The coaches were then allowed to drop back into the platform by gravity, the locomotive rejoined its train and the branch set was then ready to head back to Uppingham

Fire Emergency

Emergencies on the railway might easily call for some unusual working but every effort was made to try to anticipate what special equipment might be required. The old Lancashire & Yorkshire Railway, for example, kept a dedicated train at its Horwich Works for use in the case of fires on railway property. It consisted of a 2-4-2T tank locomotive, a flat wagon with three-plank sides and a six-wheel composite van brake. A Merryweather fire engine was carried on the wagon.

Flat wagons were also provided by British Rail (Western) for use by the fire services in the event of a fire in the Severn Tunnel. There were two Carflat wagons at Pilning and a Carflat and a Weltrol at Severn Tunnel Junction. For tunnel examinations a powerful searchlight was also stabled at Pilning.

The Fourpenny Rope

The 1840 London & Blackwall (L&B)Railway acquired this label because it was worked by rope haulage and because 4d was one of its principal fares. Running from Fenchurch Street to the Thames at Blackwall, the railway was promoted to secure a share of the rapidly expanding steamer business to the pleasure resorts downstream. By taking the train to Blackwall and joining a steamer at Brunswick Wharf passengers would save time by cutting across the neck of the huge bend in the river and avoid the shipping congestion further upstream.

Trains on the double track, 3.6-mile route were worked by rope haulage throughout, power being provided by engines and winding drums located before the final rise into each terminus. There were five intermediate stations and a fleet of six-wheeled coaches with an end platform for the men who operated the uncoupling and rope grip apparatus. Twelve such

This early photograph of the Docklands Light Railway shows a train crossing a viaduct originally built by the London & Blackwall Railway.

coaches were in use on each line, one at each intermediate station before the journey began and seven at the two starting points. As each of the single coaches neared the Minories or Blackwall engine it released the rope and ran forward until braked to a stand. The group of seven 'slipped' one vehicle at each intermediate station with the other two going through. The line worked reasonably well once wire hawsers had replaced the hemp ropes and continued in this way for nine years before locomotives took over.

One of the less attractive jobs on the L&B was that of the men who stood chest deep in small cavities near each winding house and made sure that the cables were guided smoothly onto the drums.

Reversals

A route noted for the times its trains had to reverse direction was the coastal one north from Scarborough to Whitby and beyond. Its services departed from Platform 1A at Scarborough and reversed at Londesborough Road before heading northwards. At Whitby another reversal was then necessary to get from the high level viaduct down to the sea level station terminus. In the same area some special scenic excursion trains from Hull to Scarborough involved reversals at Driffield, Malton and Whitby while some trains between Middlesbrough and Scarborough involved no less than five reversals, two at Guisborough, two at Whitby and a final one at Scarborough. Any disoriented passengers could, if need be, recover with a short rest on Scarborough's noted 200-person platform seat.

EIGHT

ENTERPRISE

Railways were closely regulated right from the start but the tight restrictions on rates and fares did not prevent them showing a great deal of commercial initiative. This became increasing apparent after the end of the nineteenth century when advertising posters first began to appear and from then on the variety of services and facilities increased steadily. The GWR, for example, introduced its first motor bus services from Helston to the Lizard and from Penzance to Marazion in 1903 and by 1931 was offering an air service between Plymouth and Cardiff.

Water

Railways no longer have to supply water to fill the tanks and tenders of steam locomotives nor to deliver drinking water by train to remote level crossings and signal boxes. Water still matters greatly, though, and filling carriages alone is a massive undertaking.

Water proved a great challenge when building the Severn Tunnel, especially when construction work breached the 'Great Spring'. This still flows through the tunnel today but is now contained by pumping. Together with the water draining in from adjoining land the volume pumped can exceed 20 million gallons a day and its sale to local industries brings in some very useful revenue.

Sea water was at one period conveyed in barrels from Lowestoft to London for use in the brine baths of the Great Eastern Hotel at Liverpool Street station. Another movement of brine passed from Droitwich for use in the baths of the hotel linked to Great Malvern station.

More recently Merseyrail encountered a major problem when some local industrial users ceased production and the water they had been using caused a 2–4m rise in the water table inside the tunnel approach to central Liverpool. The inundation overwhelmed the tunnel drainage system and began to corrode rail fittings and signal equipment. It cost £284,000 to

Before the installation of modern electrical pumps at the Sudbrook Pumping Station these massive steam-powered beam engines kept the Severn Tunnel dry.

At Great Malvern what was once Lady Foley's private waiting room now serves refreshments. The covered walkway from the platform to the former railway hotel is no longer used, nor is the archway through which coal was brought in.

put matters right and install pumps and pipes to channel the water out to Georges Dock pumping station.

Pooling

The scramble for traffic was keenest in areas served by more than one railway, places like Peterborough where the Great Eastern, Great Northern, Midland

and London & North Western companies all had depots. Around the end of the nineteenth century the Midland, in particular, had a reputation for aggressive canvassing and at Peterborough this took the form of special deals with the farmers of the fenland to the east and arrangements to bring their traffic by barge along the local waterways to the Midland's wharf. The Great Northern was extremely concerned by this development.

Grain, hay, straw and root crops were the main traffics in dispute but the Midland offer of lending sacks to farmers free and then charging only 1s a ton for the actual water collection represented a high inducement. From Peterborough to destination the company applied the standard public rates so that the GNR had no grounds for reporting them to the Railway & Canal Traffic Commission, despite the fact that barging from the more distant places like Vermuden's Drain or the Old Bedford River would have cost the MR four times what it was charging the sender. The Midland also barged some traffic into its depot at Lincoln.

Moved to protect the existing business barged into Peterborough and depots on the Ramsey North Branch the Great Northern retaliated by meeting the collection barging costs themselves and merely invoicing the sender as if the traffic had been put on rail at his local station. The Great Eastern was also affected by this scramble for traffic and, to a lesser extent, the LNW.

The rating arrangements got more and more complicated so that, in the end, the four railways met and agreed to end subsidised lighterage and 'pool' all receipts on the traffic involved with a division of income based on their individual carryings in 1899–1901. Along with other pools like the Liverpool Timber and the Norfolk & Suffolk Livestock examples, the 'Fenland Lighterage Pool' was then to last well into the post-Grouping era. In its case the LNER paid out a lot more than it got in but reasoned that withdrawal could affect other pools where the division of earnings worked out more to its advantage.

Shopping

To encourage travel for shopping purposes railways introduced cheap fares on market days and, in the case of the Great Eastern Railway, went as far as offering half price shopping seasons to the wives of holders of London season tickets. Those living in remote GWR areas could even have their weekly grocery order delivered by train. They could order from a Barkers or Harrods catalogue which arrived by post on Monday, post the order on Tuesday and pick it up from the local station on the Thursday.

Clerical Services

After successfully competing in touch typing speed trials in 1910 and becoming a champion in this new skill, A.J. Sylvester was engaged by the London & North Western Railway to provide typing services on the City to City Express between Birmingham and Broad Street station, London. He was allocated a compartment and there took dictation and produced letters for the train's business clientele. Sylvester made some useful contacts while working on the train and, through these, was eventually to become Principal Private Secretary to David Lloyd George.

Dispensing Machines

At one time any station of any size used to have a tall, red, iron machine which would yield a bar of Nestlé's chocolate if you were strong enough to pull forward the metal slide which inserting a coin had released. The chocolate bars were stored in a vertical chamber and were visible through a glass panel so one could be sure that the machine was not empty. The lowest bar sat in the slide itself and was replaced by gravity once the delivery had been made and the slide returned to its normal position.

In 1930 the GWR installed chocolate machines in the corridors of sixteen main line express trains, including the Up and Down workings of the Cornish Riviera and the Torbay Express. The LNER went one better and introduced some 200 machines on its principal services to Norwich, Cromer, Hunstanton, Southend and Harwich/Parkeston Quay. Later machines catered for anyone wanting to imprint words on a metal strip. You turned the 'clock-hand' type of pointer to your chosen letter and pulled down a lever to imprint it on the strip which was then cut and delivered at the end. This fascinating process was not to be embarked upon if you were pushed for time.

A step further forward in time brings to mind a bitterly cold winter journey back from the west of England and the eagerly anticipated soup dispensing machine at Taunton station. Frozen, fumbling fingers inserted the requisite coins but anticipation turned to dismay as the precious steaming soup poured out – with the cup eventually following!

Strawberries

Strawberry traffic was so important on the Somerset branch line from Yatton to Wells that it earned this modest Mendip railway the title of 'The Strawberry Line.'

Strawberries had been carried by rail since well before the end of the nineteenth century. Back in the 1890s the Great Western and LSW companies competed fiercely for the carriage of the early crops from the area around Callington. The GWR laid on horse vans to rush the baskets of fruit into Saltash and Tavistock while the South Western even went as far as carting them to the Tamar ferry at Cotehele, across the river and then on to its station at Bere Alston which handled some 300,000 baskets in a season.

Umbrella Hire

In 1933 the LNER ran some unusual trials at Newcastle and Hull where a gent's umbrella could be hired after a deposit of 3s 6d or a lady's umbrella for 2s 6d. The deposit was refunded when the umbrella was returned less a hire fee of 2d per day.

Sight-Seeing Car

As early as 1908 the GWR operated sight-seeing tours of London using a sixteen-seat motor vehicle. This had four double seats on each side of an enclosed saloon, each pair slightly raised above those in front and provided with deep viewing windows. In the summer two trips were offered, on Tuesday and Thursdays, leaving Paddington after the 10.30 a.m. and 2.30 p.m. arrivals and returning at 1 p.m. and 5 p.m.

Advertising

Posters were used extensively on stations, hoardings and motor vehicles to bring in advertising revenue and to stimulate rail travel. At one time the M&GN even had card tickets in 'pocket' form, containing a further card advertising Spratt's biscuits.

Films

The LNER incorporated a cinema van in its King's Cross–Leeds expresses as early as June 1935. By November 1936 it had travelled 63,000 miles and been visited by 16,000 people. The LMS made extensive use of a similar vehicle, based on a converted sleeping car, for showing films of instruction to its staff. In an eight-month tour it visited sixty-eight stations and screened 572 'showings'.

In 1937 the GWR began running excursions from Bristol to Pinewood studios. On arrival passengers were filmed, given a studio tour and provided

A typical railway poster designed to stimulate holiday travel.

with tea before making their return journey. Later the BTC Film Unit produced many award-winning films itself and these were frequently shown to societies and groups to encourage party traffic bookings.

Information

Among the less well-known facilities offered by railways was a horse racing 'first' when the LNER installed two 'Fullograph' radio receivers on the Up and Down Flying Scotsman for use on Derby Day 1929. These not only allowed the race result to be rubber stamped onto cards which were then distributed along the train, but also picked up three or four pictures of the Derby event itself.

In Scotland reports of bad weather in the offing were telegraphed to vulnerable locations in the Highlands while at least one pre-grouping railway posted weather forecasts in some of its northern town offices to encourage excursion bookings.

Produce

Farm produce carryings were vital to rural railways like the Great Eastern. Before the end of the nineteenth century it was offering to supply boxes at a nominal rate to farmers and market gardeners for the carriage of their goods to the London markets. In 1911 nearly 90,000 such boxes were sold by the company. Special arrangements were made for other agricultural traffics such as the large quantities of Yorkshire rhubarb carried into London and the game boxes and parcels despatched from the big estates in Scotland. Labelled with the number of brace inside and when killed, these boxes were conveyed by 'express and fast passenger trains'. Rabbits were also big business with thousands conveyed from Thetford to London, all strung on rods in special vans and surrounded by an aroma distinctive and unpleasant.

Another GER enterprise was the 'Egg and Poultry Demonstration Train' which toured East Anglia in 1916. The company also had its own farm at Bentley which supplied produce to the railway hotels and catering establishments. One GER failure was trying to set up its own fruit and vegetable market in Bishopsgate goods depot to cash in on the overcrowding at Spitalfields. The railway lost a resultant legal action but then achieved its end by opening Stratford Market depot in 1879.

The Coronation

Between the wars railways began to offer camping coaches to holidaymakers. These were carriages converted to provide self-catering accommodation and sited at stations adjacent to holiday areas. During Coronation week the LNER placed camping coaches at suitable outer London stations, charged £10 a week for their use by six occupants and provided them with free travel into London each day.

NINE

DRAMA

Drama on the rail network generally means that things are not running smoothly. It can also mean tragedy, but there is often an accompaniment of courage, ingenuity and professionalism.

Even in the sphere of drama railways maintain the element of variety. In the early days of steam there were, for example, spectacular chases when unattended engines sometimes set off on their own and had to be pursued. Bad weather often produced high drama and railways might also be the innocent victims of crime or anarchy. Less innocent were the occasions when the early railway companies took to physical violence to protect their interests or territory.

Lethal Weapon

In the terrible winter of 1947 the Settle & Carlisle line was blocked from 4 February until 19 March, the worst affected section being that between Blea Moor Tunnel and Garsdale. Class 4 0-6-0 goods engines were used in pairs with a chimney plough to try to clear the snow. The job was a rough one for the locomotives were coupled tender to tender which meant that the crew of the rear locomotive got soaked from the snow flying backwards. This was bad enough, but in one incident the plough somehow tilted and uprooted a length of rail which went up the blade, over the boiler and through the cab window of the leading engine! Fortunately it missed the crew.

Tunnel Inferno

One of BR's freight business successes was securing a large share of the movement of petroleum products to rail in 100-ton tank wagons. A train made up of thirteen of these high-capacity vehicles was on its way from ICI Haverton Hill to Glazebrook at the beginning of 1985 when it was derailed in the 2,885-yard Summit Tunnel between Todmorden and Rochdale. The mishap occurred about halfway through the tunnel and although the train crew managed to draw the locomotive and three wagons clear the two derailed wagons caught fire and created an inferno which would have been dramatic in the open but, in the confines of the tunnel, was like a vision of hell. The firemen on the scene pumped foam down the ventilation shafts and only just escaped a massive explosion which pushed temperatures up to an incredible 8,000 degrees centigrade and resulted in smoke and flames shooting out of the shafts and 200ft into the air.

Four days of fire inside the tunnel vitrified the brickwork, buckled the rails and destroyed the sleepers and power cables. It mangled and twisted the train wreckage into a hopeless shape. Despite this the 140-year-old tunnel had taken the mauling well and a massive clearance, relaying and repair effort put paid to fears that this scenic cross-Pennine route might never re-open.

Trains in the Troubles

Railways have not been immune from Northern Ireland's unhappy 'troubles'. In one case members of the Provisional IRA stopped a Dublin–Belfast freight train loaded with beer and stout and turned it into a dangerous weapon that kept the border section of the line closed for five days. This was done by loading 300lb of high explosives into two milk churns, placing them in the CIE locomotive and then stranding it in a cutting. What happened to the beer is not recorded.

In another incident a Dundalk–Adelaide goods train was hijacked and sent driverless across the border. The scheme backfired when the train stalled on a gradient and ran back the way it had come!

CIE locomotive A60R had featured in a similar action just a few days earlier. Working the 03.30 Dublin–Belfast newspaper train with a single van, it was stopped by armed men between Dundalk and the border. A telephone call was then made to Portadown station warning that the train was being sent forward loaded with explosives. People living near the station were hurriedly evacuated and the nearby urban motorway closed.

The drama reached fever pitch as it became clear that the hijacked train was on its way, heading at well over 60mph for the bridge and curve that preceded the station.

With a 15mph restriction applying on the curve disaster seemed inevitable. A60R came off the track with spectacular force, but fortunately the explosives threat was a hoax and no lives were lost.

Camping Out

As early as 1851 railways were using 'snow brooms' tied to the locomotive guard irons to brush winter snow from the line, and ingenious engineers quickly evolved a simple form of snow plough for pushing deeper snow aside. However, the elements are not always defeated easily as a Tweedmouth footplate crew were to discover when their train for Newcastle got stuck in a snow drift at Alnmouth in 1886. It was to be four days before they were rescued during which time the passengers and crew lived off kippers and rabbits, supplemented by melted snow laced from the driver's bottle of whisky. The locomotive firebox supplied heat and the means to cook the rabbits they caught. The kippers came from the luggage of a group of fisher lasses who had been on their way to Scarborough.

Being Prepared

Bad weather in the Scottish Highlands is always a challenge for rail operators. One of the precautions regularly used was to place an emergency hamper on winter services on the Oban line and those from Inverness to Glasgow, Wick/Thurso and the Kyle of Lochalsh. Each hamper contained food and drink for fifty passengers for 24 hours plus blankets and basic heating, lighting and cooking facilities.

Brunel Vindicated

The Western Region of BR had cause to be thankful for the broad gauge legacy of extra space between its running lines when it heard of a 1980 mishap on the East Coast Main Line.

When a vandal threw a stone at the 15.35 Kings Cross–Newcastle High Speed Train as it passed through Hitchin it just broke the outer glass of one window. Unfortunately the inner pane then succumbed to suction when an Up HST from Leeds passed and fragments of glass ricocheted between the two HSTs and also damaged more windows on a following Up service from Cleethorpes. The WR did not incur that high cost of window strengthening which the Eastern had to face.

Third Time Unlucky

Petrol tankers were unheard of when the railway bridge from Sharpness across the River Severn towards Lydney was opened in 1879, yet it was to be river tankers which caused its closure eighty-one years later. Currents, tides, winds, shoals and bends make river navigation a tricky business at the best of times and ships have run into railway bridges on many occasions, especially the swing bridges of Yorkshire and East Anglia. The exceptional tides encountered on the Severn make it a particularly difficult river to navigate but, in the light of the large number of vessels using the river and the canal link on from Sharpness to Gloucester Docks, it is curious that tankers should have damaged the Severn Railway Bridge on no less than three occasions.

The first of these accidents occurred in 1938 when a tug and three tanker barges were swept onto one of the piers, wrapped their towing hawser around it and capsized. On that occasion the bridge damage was not great, but in the late evening of 25 October 1960 something much more serious happened. Two motor vessels, *Arkendale H* and *Wastdale H,* were nearing Sharpness in low fog when they collided and, unable to break the suction and separate, were hurled onto Pier 17 of the bridge by a fast moving tide. There was a great explosion, fire shot high into the air and the pier, together with its adjacent spans, collapsed into the waters below. Five crew members from the tankers died.

While reconstruction of the bridge was still being considered, the *coup de grâce* was administered by another tanker. This was the *BP Explorer* which capsized while heading up river to Sharpness, was carried beyond the bridge by the tide and then came back on the ebb to smash into Pier 20 and close the railway bridge forever.

In the period between the closure of the Severn Railway Bridge and its eventual demolition the local railway staff had to maintain red warning lights at the breach, a pretty onerous task on a rough windy day. Removing the lights became something of a sport for the local lads who would dare one another to make the perilous night journey along the damaged and desolate structure and return with a trophy. One consequent difficulty arose from the fact that if a lamp

The swing bridge over the North Docks branch at Sharpness, pictured here in the 1980s, was the last portion of the Severn Railway Bridge works to survive.

blew out it was a traffic staff job to relight it, but if the lamp was stolen it was a matter for the British Transport Police. Some highly entertaining debates took place between the two departments before an elected victim could be persuaded to turn out and walk the bare track over the river to remedy the matter.

Flood Waters

The author's introduction to the devastation caused by flood waters occurred in the winter of 1946–47 while relieving a post at Hardingham station on the Norwich–Dereham line. Heavy snow necessitated the use of a gang of unrepatriated Italian PoWs to dig out an Up train and the subsequent thaw was to put much of the Norfolk railway system under water. Despite the passage of over half a century two memories from this time are still crystal clear. One is of the journey home to Norwich as the thaw set in when the normal train noises were drowned by the sound of swollen streams rushing beneath the track, an eerie and ominous feeling in a dark and threatening landscape. The other is of a journey over the newly opened Fenland stretch of railway between Brandon and Ely. Apart from a few trees and isolated farmhouses the waters stretched to the horizon.

There were severe floods in the north in 1948 when six days of steady rain was followed by a twenty-four-hour downpour which lifted the waters of the River Tweed and the Eye Water by over 15ft. Water, mud and landslides washed out miles of railway track and dozens of structures and completely cut off East Coast access to Edinburgh either via Berwick or Carlisle. With thirteen routes east of Peebles and north of St Boswells affected, all services to Scotland had to be routed over the West Coast Main Line.

The year 1953 will always be remembered for the high tides and severe gales which caused great floods along the East Coast and had such a disastrous effect on Canvey Island. Miles and miles of railway track were washed out and a huge programme of rerouting services and, later, rebuilding became necessary. Among the many dramatic incidents were the Harwich–Zeebrugge train ferry vessel *Essex* being lifted high on the tide and badly damaging the 120-ton bridge ramp at Harwich, and one of the Humber ferries being swept from its mooring and crashing into the pontoon at New Holland Pier station. To add to the main area of damage the paddler's funnel somehow got tangled up with a signal gantry.

There was further drama around the coast of Norfolk. Late in the evening of 31 January Breydon Water burst its banks and flooded first Yarmouth South Town and then Vauxhall station. The north bank of Oulton Broad had already given way to submerge Lowestoft station and depot to a depth of 3ft and water had rushed up the harbour line route at Wells to do the same there. In north

Norfolk passengers on the 7.27 p.m. service from Hunstanton suffered an ordeal which started when the train ran into a wall of water and a floating bungalow thudded into the engine smokebox and damaged the brake pipe. The water continued to rise until it was level with the carriage seats and had doused the locomotive fire. Six hours in darkness followed with debris crashing into the stranded coaches as the train staff laboured to keep spirits up and find a way out of their fearful situation. Eventually temporary repairs were effected and enough wood accumulated to relight the fire and raise just enough steam to reverse back to Hunstanton.

Chase and Capture

A newspaper report of 1849 carried a report of a collision near Gravesend in which the engine and carriage of a special train was run into by a ballast train in thick fog. Just before the carriage was smashed to pieces the driver of the special had leapt from the footplate to avoid injury. Unfortunately the impact resulted in the driverless engine setting off alone and leaving the switchman at Gravesend no choice but to direct it onto the main line if a second collision, with an Up train in the station platform, was to be avoided. The account continues:

A train leaving Norwich for Cambridge in 1936. This line followed the course of the River Yare and its tributaries westward from Trowse, and is still liable to flooding.

1960 brought flooding on the main line through Hele & Bradninch.

The moment it [the engine] had passed, the information was telegraphed up the line to the chairman and superintendent of the railway. The latter immediately proceeded on an express engine down the line, and soon after his departure the telegraph brought the account of its having passed the Woolwich station. Under the personal directions of the chairman and other officials at the London-bridge station, preparations were immediately made for its reception at the station, if it should arrive there at speed, so as to prevent any ill consequences ensuing beyond injury to the engine itself. Sleepers were placed upon the road, and an engine was fixed there as a buttress to receive it. The special engine carrying the superintendent met the runaway engine between the Bricklayers' Arms station and the New-cross-bridge, then backed to follow it, crossing at the junction on the same line as the runaway which it pursued and overtook, running into it at speed. The driver of this engine gallantly sprang from the pursuing engine on to the runaway and immediately obtained control over it, and the two engines thus arrived in perfect control at the London-bridge terminus.

When the Snow Lay Round About…

Railway managers were not just desk jockeys but could, and did, get involved with the sharp end of the business, as these words of Hugh Jenkins, then Divisional Manager at Birmingham, express:

It was bitterly cold and a blizzard was blowing. The passengers aboard the Euston express were aware that they were making particularly slow progress, and that they had been held up outside Rugby for many long minutes. The main line through Kilsby Tunnel was closed temporarily. Icicles were hanging down from the ventilator shafts like frozen spears and needed to be removed before safe working could resume. The decision was taken to divert our express via Northampton, but no trains had used the Northampton loop for well over two hours and there was some uncertainty about the exact conditions. I joined the cab of the locomotive for this leg of the journey.

The driver made steady progress in a heavy blizzard, experiencing near 'whiteout' conditions once or twice. We then came to an open stretch of line where powdery snow had drifted across the track. For over a hundred yards we had the uncanny sensation of travelling by train across a snow-covered field. The track in front of us was completely invisible. Then it reappeared; we were safely through. Next we began hitting a series of separate snowdrifts, with sudden judders and constant vibration. Suddenly we lost all power. The snow had been forced into the traction motors of our Class 86 electric locomotive. We were stranded; it was obviously 'the wrong kind of snow!' Eventually, arrangements were made for another train to couple up behind and push us to Northampton.

For safety reasons the assisting train had to be accompanied forward to effect the rescue due to the poor visibility at the time. The guard and I walked back a mile in the blizzard and guided the second train forward. After coupling up we rejoined the first train. I then got on the public system, introduced myself, and gave the passengers a factual account of what had happened and why. As the guard and I walked back through the train we were given a spontaneous round of applause. I wondered how we had been recognised until I realised that we looked like two snowmen, complete with very red noses!

Ill-Fated Venture

It seemed an excellent idea to shorten the rail route for West Cumberland ore to the Scottish ironworks and the promoters of the Solway Junction Railway (SJR) set up their scheme for a short railway across the Solway Firth confident in the expectation of earning rich rewards from carrying the ore. Following incorporation in 1864 work started on the new line, but it ran into awful problems in crossing a swamp on the southern approach to the viaduct across the Firth. The viaduct itself was a daunting task for it needed 193 cast-iron spans and was the longest of its day. It was six years before the route was fully opened by which time the traffic prospects had been depressed by the building of new ironworks near the ore deposits.

The 1,940-yard viaduct was a source of constant worry for the SJR management. Water started leaking into some of the columns which then burst during a severe frost in 1876. Five years later another prolonged cold spell froze the waters of the Firth and brought disaster when they thawed. For four days huge blocks of ice rushed downstream on the swollen waters and crashed into the piers of the bridge, sometimes wedging themselves fast until smashed into pieces by those following. It took three years to raise the necessary funds and then repair the bridge but things were never the same afterwards.

Bristol Marooned

A never-to-be-forgotten memory is that of standing in the West of England Division's Control Office in the former Bristol & Exeter Railway headquarters building at Bristol Temple Meads, as a period of sustained heavy rain in July 1968 gradually flooded all the railway routes converging on the city. What gave the occasion a special reality was the vivid process of seeing

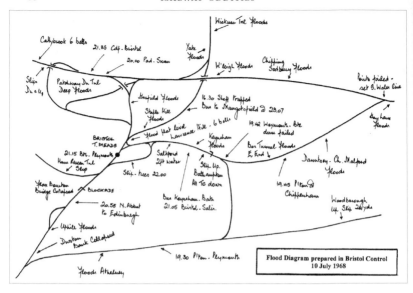

Flood Diagram prepared in Bristol Control
10 July 1968

the information coming in from stations and signal boxes being entered on a rough hand-drawn diagram of the railways in the area. Implacably the diagram became covered with notes of strandings, floodings and equipment failures until it bore a very real resemblance to a battlefield.

Head-on Collision

One of the most terrible accidents ever to occur in Norfolk was a head-on collision between two trains on Thursday 10 September 1874. It took place just outside Norwich on a single line near Thorpe village and involved the 5 p.m. passenger train from London to Yarmouth via Norwich and the Up London mail from Yarmouth and Lowestoft via Reedham.

By the evening that fateful day the weather became stormy and a high wind was blowing. North of Ipswich the crew of the 5 p.m. express from Bishopsgate to Yarmouth were losing the fight to maintain schedule with a small engine and a fourteen-coach train and would clearly be late into Norwich where 2-4-0 locomotive No.218 was waiting to take the train forward. By the time the London train arrived at Norwich at 9.23 p.m. the thirteen-coach Up mail train from Yarmouth, headed by Sinclair Single No.54, was already forty-three minutes into its journey towards the dead end station beside the river at Norwich. The coroner was later to comment on railwaymen being expected to work 'as many hours as human nature can stand' and long hours on duty may have been the reason for a misunderstanding between Stationmaster Sproule, the day and night inspectors at Norwich and their telegraph clerk. Whatever the cause, Night Inspector Cooper called up the mail while Day Inspector Robson authorised the Down express to leave. The two trains were now heading towards one another on a single line. The mistake was quickly realised and a 'Stop Mail' message sent over the Cooke & Wheatstone telegraph to Stationmaster Platford at Brundall, but the terrible and hopeless reply came back, 'Mail Left'.

As the full horror of the situation dawned on the Norwich staff the twenty-year-old engine of the Down train had worked its train speed up to 25mph as it crossed the first bridge over the River Yare. Just a couple of miles away the single wheeler was running nicely at around 35mph. Overhead the skies were split with rolling thunder and flashes of lightning which briefly illuminated the work going on to convert the Reedham and Cromer single lines into double track.

Just beyond the second Yare bridge the trains met with a fearful crash which shook the neighbourhood and piled up the wooden coaches in a tangle of rain-soaked wreckage. In the darkness the train crews were the first to die and many passengers were killed or fearfully injured. Some miraculously escaped like the couple who moved to a rear carriage because they had been offended by fellow passengers in the leading vehicle, and the lady who was thrown into the trees of a nearby garden but escaped with just bruising and some loss of dignity.

Soon rescuers were on the scene, including local people, railway staff, and Dr Hill and his colleagues from the nearby Thorpe mental hospital. The noise of the storm, the roar of escaping steam and the piteous cries of the injured created a nightmare shrouded in darkness but fires were quickly lit using the scattered wreckage as fuel and the long night of succour began. The medical people were tireless, carrying out some operations on the spot and arranging hasty bandaging of those who could be moved to the adjacent hospital. The railwaymen showed their usual devotion to duty with Guard Ellis of the Mail, although dazed and injured from the disintegration of his van, still insisting on finding a cart to convey his mail bags to the post office before he would accept attention.

If the weather had not been so awful the London express might have been on time, if the work on doubling the lines had been passed for use by the Board of Trade, if the Norwich railway staff had not been tired and overworked… the tragedy might not have happened. Conversely, if the two trains had met on the river bridge or if there had not been a hospital nearby things might even have been worse. As it was twenty-five people lost their lives and seventy-three were injured in this sad piece of railway drama.

TEN

BARELY BELIEVABLE

You would think that the railway activity, by reason of its fixed infrastructure, comprehensive regulation and its culture of safety and service, would hold few surprises. But you would need to think again. Being a complex industry there is more scope for the out-of-the-ordinary. Even so, stealing a station and a complaint about a shortage of fairies do put a strain on the imagination!

The Snow Jet

One of the great enemies of the railway system has always been heavy, drifting snow, especially on lines with deep cuttings. By coincidence heavy snowfalls in early 1947 provided an excellent opportunity to test out some original thinking about the problem. If snow could not be forced aside by a snowplough, perhaps the solution was to melt it. Everyone knew that the Army used flame throwers, so why not borrow one? Nice try, but first experiments with a military flame thrower set fire to everything combustible in the vicinity and caused so much damage to sleepers and fencing that something less ferocious had to be found!

After discussions between the LNER and the appropriate government department, the National Gas Turbine Laboratory was called in to run an experiment using, of all things, aircraft jet engines. Two huge gas turbine engines were fitted with long exhaust tubes and chained side by side on a Conflat wagon with the exhausts pointing backwards and slightly downwards in the manner of depressed gun barrels. A small train was then made up by adding a tank wagon of kerosene fuel, a tool and mess van, a brake van and finally the propelling locomotive.

There was plenty of snow to choose from around Peterborough and there was also a trial at Louth on the Grimsby line. Some success with shifting powdery snow was reported but the monster was hard to control with just a fuel throttle and damage continued to occur. George Dow, then public relations officer of the LNER, wrote, 'with certain types of snow these turbines are quite effective, but when ice was encountered the results were not entirely satisfactory' – a truly smooth PR statement.

In an article in *Steam World* High Dyke branch signalmen Peter Keys described more graphically a visit from the 'snow jet' train. It had been worked up from New England and then reversed onto the iron ore branch to help clear a snow blockage there. Everyone had been warned to take cover while the deafening contraption was spitting hot exhaust. Again it made short work of the loose snow but 'it also shattered some of the windows, blew down the lineside fencing and left gaping holes between the sleepers where the ash bed had been blown away!' No more was heard of the idea.

Railway Chairman in a Dilemma

This was the headline for a report in the *Doncaster Chronicle & Farmers' Journal* of 19 October 1849. The report itself recorded:

> At a meeting of the Dundrum Railway Company, in Ireland, a few days since, it was moved that the chairman should be thrown out of the window; an amendment was moved that he should be thrown down the stairs; the original motion was, however, adopted and was about to be carried into effect when a general fight ensued.
>
> The directors and shareholders appeared next day at the police office.

Rail Chief is Sidetracked

A newspaper report dated 12 October 1971 carried this heading and began:

> The chairman of India's nationalised railways, Mr B.C.Ganguli, 57, spent a second day yesterday with his wife and family in a carriage at No.3 platform of a New Delhi suburban station.

Apparently Mr Ganguli had been having 'policy differences' with the Indian Government railway minister, Mr Hanumanthaiya. These had become so serious that the minister had stripped the railway chairman of his duties and ordered an immediate end to the latter's tour of the system in his official carriage. Chairman Ganguli's train had only got three miles outside the capital when the order was implemented by detaching his saloon and shunting it into one of the suburban station's platforms. There he steadfastly refused to leave the train and go home.

An accommodation was eventually reached between the two parties but not before the railway chairman had spent five days marooned at the suburban station. His coach was air conditioned and he had the company of his family so the hardship may not have been too great.

Railway Station 'Stolen'

Another newspaper report recorded a case heard in Wakefield Crown Court in 1972 in which a Dewsbury man pleaded not guilty to stealing stone, timber and metal after demolishing a closed station without permission. As the prosecution put it, 'What it really comes to is that last August in effect he stole Cleckheaton station.'

Cleckheaton had lost its passenger services in 1965 with freight facilities being withdrawn four years later. British Rail then contracted with a Leeds firm who were to get £2,383 for clearing the site plus the proceeds from selling the materials. When they turned up most of the station and its materials had gone! The man responsible apparently paid out a bond, hired machinery and worked on the site for three weeks after agreeing to undertake its clearance for another firm which no one had subsequently been able to trace. He was duped and left sadly out of pocket, but at least the court cleared him of the theft charges.

The Crown Street Affair

Something rather more dramatic in the arena of unwelcome station clearances took place in Carlisle on a Saturday in March 1849. Behind it lay a typical George Hudson intrigue, played out through the Maryport & Carlisle (M&C) Railway which had become part of the Hudson 'empire' in 1848. The M&C trains were using a station at Crown Street as their Carlisle terminus but the site was needed for the new Lancaster & Carlisle (L&C) Railway's station and had been included in that company's authorising Act. Hudson was asking £100,000 for Crown Street against a figure of £7,005 offered by the L&C! The courts ruled in favour of the latter but the M&C remained intransigent despite an order from Carlisle's high sheriff.

On the morning of Saturday 17 March 1849 matters came dramatically to a head. The day started off normally enough at Crown Street but midway between the morning and midday trains normality was rudely shattered. First the under sheriff appeared and formally gave possession of the site to the Lancaster & Carlisle Co. whose resident engineer then waived his handkerchief as a signal to bring a horde of 150 workmen charging onto the site. Using horses and drag chains they quickly ripped up the wooden platforms and loaded the debris into carts. The running rails were levered up and the lime and coal depot then subjected to the brutal demolition process. Attention next turned to the station buildings where the bemused clerks just had time to gather up their books before their workplace was also converted to rubble. Thoughtfully, Superintendent Bibby of the L&C's police had sent a man to halt the train due at 11.30 a.m. and tell the astonished driver that his destination no longer existed!

The Maryport & Carlisle Co. went back to court and lost and, impudently, Hudson submitted a claim for compensation over the Crown Street affair, but his star was now waning and the Maryport & Carlisle first tidied up its chaotic affairs and then reached an agreement with its former adversary for M&C trains to use the new Citadel station.

Private Enterprise

On Monday 13 September 1971 a coal train was derailed at Flax Bourton just south of Bristol. Several wagons came off the rails and overturned, scattering coal over both tracks of the WR main line to Taunton. All the normal emergencies arrangements were put in place by the West of England Division's control office, including the hiring of coaches from Turners of Bristol for use in providing an alternative service for passengers while the clearance of the wreckage took place.

The north end of the original Crown Street site eventually became the Up bay of Carlisle Citadel station and is pictured with empty coaches and Class 8 shunting locomotives.

Unlike the Flax Bourton scene in September 1971 everything in this modern view is normal as a train from Bristol speeds through the site of the old station on its way to Weston-super-Mare.

The replacement coach service between Bristol and Weston-super-Mare worked without a hitch, helped by the tireless efforts of a young man 'from the Area Manager's office at Bristol'. He clearly knew the normal service by heart and, after discussing the bus schedules with Turners, spent a lot of time directing the drivers, making sure passengers boarded the right vehicle and liaising with station staff over the whole operation. He seemed to be decisive and tireless.

On Day 3, with the bus service running well, our hero turned up at the derailment site in a hired, chauffeur-driven car to discuss the clearance operation with the civil engineering staff. Urging the need for greater speed in moving the spilled coal he made arrangements for it to be offered at 25p a hundredweight to anyone who could collect it for themselves. Providing receipts and promising that the money would go to the railway orphanage, he had plenty of takers. One of the derailed wagons was also offered to a scrap merchant for £25.

Some delayed passengers from Bristol to Newport later benefited when a luxury coach was ordered for them but the coach company began to have its suspicions and decided to check the bona fides of the man 'from the Area Manager's office'. There no one had heard of him and the British Transport Police were called in. Incredulous officers made their enquiries and discovered that he was a complete impostor whose only credentials were many years of dedicated train spotting!

Unfortunately the train spotter's incredible activities proved more than just a quixotic adventure for he was later found to have defrauded several groups in other parts of the country and eventually paid for his audacity with a prison sentence.

An Odd Complaint

Christmas is supposed to be a season of goodwill but one passenger on a Nene Valley Railway 'Santa Special' in 1978 seemed to think himself hard done by and complained to the railway and the local consumer protection department about his outing with his son. Apparently he had no quarrel with the festive train journey, the mince pies or the glass of sherry, but was distinctly aggrieved because, while the NVR posters had clearly promised that Father Christmas would be attended by elves, pixies and fairies, not one fairy had actually put in an appearance!

Public Proposal

Absence may well make the heart grow fonder, but rarely with the rapid consequences reported in January 1996, and rarely in such a busy railway setting. The leading lady in this incident, Nicola, and her hero, Scott, had just said a fond farewell at London Victoria station. She had boarded a Gatwick Express service in order to catch a flight to Aberdeen, but Scott found himself so upset by the separation that he enlisted railway staff to get a desperate message to his girlfriend. With the help of a Victoria Welcome Host, the train conductor and the Gatwick station announcer, Nicola was greeted on alighting with the message:

Scott H wishes Miss Nicola T, flying to Aberdeen, to marry him.

The Gatwick information desk was next to feature in this extraordinary drama when the young lady, weeping happy tears, identified herself and said the answer was 'yes'. One telephone call back to Victoria and BR's brief excursion into the Cupid business was completed with satisfaction all round.

The New Trousers

When Carlos Mendoza, an itinerant musician, was apprehended in Bury St Edmunds in 1919 he was wearing an unusual pair of trousers: one leg of which was red, the other green. He subsequently told the Court that a dog had ripped his old trousers to shreds leaving him with only an overcoat to protect him from the bitter January weather. Cold and in desperation he broke into a lineside hut at Westley, GER, stole two signal flags and made them up into trousers. Neither Mendoza's misfortune nor his colourful solution saved him from being sentenced to a month's hard labour.

Delay with a Difference

On 19 February 1982 the 7.35 p.m. from Waterloo to Weymouth Quay was halted on the quay tramway section in Weymouth because the flange gap on a section of the line had been filled in with concrete, presumably as a result of some thoughtless building work. It was over an hour before local permanent way staff could chip the concrete out and allow the train to proceed.

Royal Travel

The provision of special rolling stock for British royal trains also extended to the continent and in 1883 a large twelve-wheel royal saloon was shipped to Calais where it was kept in a special building between journeys. Later, King

A London & North Western Railway postcard
depicts a royal train carriage and its interior.

Edward VII was travelling in this coach when an anarchist tried to assassinate
him in Belgium.

Occasionally there were other moments of 'royal' drama, like the one
resulting from the South Eastern Railway's smart run while conveying the
Shah of Persia to Windsor. The speed so upset the Shah that he demanded
the immediate execution of the train driver!

Another departure from the normal simple, decorous and precise
arrangements for trains travelling under 'Deepdene' or 'Deepcar' codes
occurred when the North British Railway carried Queen Victoria northwards
after her opening of the Royal Border Bridge in 1850. To impress their royal
passenger the NBR repainted its royal engine in the royal Stewart tartan.

Wagon Harpooned

Soon after the opening of the Bristol & Exeter Railway, a private wharf on the
River Parrett was linked to the new line at Dunball by a short horse tramway
so that coal brought over from South Wales and the Forest of Dean could be
distributed by rail in Somerset and Devon. Wharf and tramway were taken over
by the B&E and relaid as a thirty-six-chain, mixed-gauge line in 1869.

In its heyday as many as thirty trows and ketches brought coal in for
unloading to truck at the wharf. This was a dirty job and not without the
occasional mishap; none, though, quite like the incident with the *Charles* late

on a stormy day just before the First World War. A strong wind led to the vessel dragging her anchor and being driven, helpless, straight for the wall of the wharf. In the inevitable collision the *Charles* not only smashed her bow section but stuck her bowsprit through a coal wagon waiting to be loaded.

The railway staff near the wharf siding had to jump clear quickly, but then watched in astonishment as the *Charles* rebounded into the main river and sank, taking the impaled wagon down with it. The wreckage was later salvaged and auctioned.

Train Robbery

The Great Train Robbery of August 1963 produced a haul of £2.5 million for the thieves, but a copycat affair in 1989 netted only six bags of newspapers, and Polish ones at that! The thieves had interfered with the signalling to halt a Brighton to London Bridge parcels train at Mertham and made its driver hand over his keys at gunpoint. They were then in such a hurry to escape in a waiting car on the M25 that they grabbed the wrong cargo.

After the earlier robbery BR had gone to great lengths to ensure that there would be no souvenirs of the Royal Mail coach involved. It was broken up and burned at a Norwich scrapyard under very tight security arrangements so that the event could not be glamourised.

The Lapthorn vessel *Hoo Plover* unloads coal at the former railway wharf at Dunball in 1999. Back in the 1880s it would have been loaded to wagon and sent on to Devon destinations on Broad Gauge Train No.80.

Leprechauns?

Although its 12.5-mile line was opened in 1868 the Parsonstown &
Portumna Bridge Railway (P&PBR) did not last long and its extension
across the River Shannon to reach Portumna itself never got built. After
closure the infrastructure of the P&PBR just seemed to disappear, buildings,
bridges, the lot. Leprechauns were blamed.

1926 Strike

Newspapers were badly affected by the strike but most tried to struggle on
even though some editions were reduced to a small single sheet. To help fill
the information gap the LNER produced six issues of *LNER News*, the last
one containing the following item:

> THE LIMIT
> A large covered motor charabanc labelled 'London – Bradford – Leeds' drew
> up in front of the King's Cross Booking Office plying for passengers. The driver
> was informed that King's Cross is still a railway station and he was trespassing on
> L.N.E.R. Company's premises. He moved towards a neo-gothic station hard-by!

Over the Rimram

A 1952 advertisement in a railway magazine celebrated the completion
of the forty-arch Welwyn Viaduct over the River Rimram. The text
commemorated not only the new route to Scotland but also the use of
the viaduct by Blondin as a 'practice ground for his celebrated tightrope
feats across Niagara, the parapet being much narrower than it is now'. His
'passenger' was a local worthy, the redoubtable Squire Dering. The picture
accompanying the article showed Blondin using stilts.

The Incredible Fraud

Largely due to its own negligence the Great Northern Railway was the
victim of an outrageous fraud which cost the infant company nearly a
quarter of a million pounds.

The fraudster was Leonard Redpath, whom the GNR engaged as a clerk
in the Registrar's department in 1846 despite a chequered employment career
which included being dismissed for embezzlement and bankruptcy. Over the
next eight years Redpath not only robbed his employers of £120,000 and

lent some of it back to them at 4.5 per cent interest but so deceived the railway that it increased his salary three times and promoted him to clerk in charge. All this time Redpath was creating and selling fictitious stock, but no one seemed to question how he could afford his extravagant lifestyle involving luxury homes, several servants and lavish entertaining.

By 1854 something was clearly amiss, but another two years went by before he was put under pressure to explain the discrepancies. Eventually he was brought to trial and sentenced to transportation but the railway had to obtain Parliamentary powers to purchase and cancel the false stock. The cost of doing so, plus dividend payments and prosecution expenses, amounted to a staggering £244,000.

Added Protection

One of the many suggestions made for improving safety on early railways was one for hanging large bags of wool at the front and rear of trains and between the carriages to minimise the effect of a collision. A part of this concept did actually pass into the practice of one or two companies who had dummy vans attached at the back of trains which were vulnerable to rear end impact because of the short headway between one train and the next.

Inspection Result

The West of England Division of BR(W) stretched from Worcester to Penzance so a working tour of its various areas using the civil engineer's inspection saloon had several compensations for the long day and considerable effort involved in a thorough examination of local operating and commercial activity. The coach had a conference area at one end and a viewing saloon at the other with a kitchen in between, from which the travelling steward served refreshments to the railway officers and the civic, trade and other guests who were invited to join them for lunch. Taken at a suitable stopping point on a scenic part of the railway this was both a pleasant and a commercially useful event.

The working part of the journey would involve the officers from the various disciplines making key decisions on site, checking that local equipment and practices were functioning as they should and coming up with ideas for improvement or economy. Occasionally there were unexpected dividends, such as the time when a stop was made at an unstaffed station to replenish the on-board provisions from the adjacent pub, where it was discovered that the two brothers running it were still on the payroll as the station's early and late turn porters!

ELEVEN

STATIONS AND DEPOTS

At one time any sizeable community had its own railway station, usually with a goods yard adjacent in which there would be yard sidings, a goods shed, a crane and an end or side dock of some sort. Smaller communities might just have a single-platform halt, while big cities were often served by several companies, each with its own station and depot.

In addition to these conventional railway stations and depots there were marshalling yards, engine sheds, workshops large and small, carriage cleaning depots and many other locations which fulfilled special functions that rarely came to public notice. With locations so varied and numerous some unusual and curious practices were bound to exist.

The Unsung Whitemoor

The LNER was extremely proud of its pioneering mechanised marshalling yard beside the GN&GE Joint Line at Whitemoor, just north of March. There the company opened the vast Up side complex in March 1929, with the Down side following four years later when extra accommodation was also added to the locomotive depot at the south end. The two main yards each had reception and sorting siding groups and could handle 1,000 wagons on every shift by shunting separated 'cuts' over a hump, then to run by gravity down through the electrically controlled main points and via hydraulic retarders into the right siding for their onward journey.

Although less well known the original Norwood Yard survived within the new layout and was redesigned to handle the wagons unsuitable for mechanical shunting, such as those carrying livestock or fragile goods, and to undertake a whole variety of other odd jobs which would have held up the routine in the main yards. Norwood also built up a reputation for speed and skill, both vital qualities during the hectic months of the local Cambridgeshire fruit season when growers demanded the latest possible

The hump shunting signal is off in Whitemoor Down yard on 9 May 1967 and a 'cut' of seven mineral wagons has just entered the retarders.

time for loading but needed their produce to get to the northern markets early enough to command the best prices.

In the 1950s Norwood was booked to handle twenty or more trains a day but the really hectic period started early in the evening with seven trains of urgent fruit traffic from the Wisbech & Upwell Tramway and other local branches arriving between 5.38 p.m. and 6.33 p.m. Their incoming vans had to be marshalled ready for four trains leaving between 7.22 p.m. and 8.15 p.m., without detriment to the two parcels trains despatched at 6.30 p.m. and a third at 8 p.m. Most nights there would also be a few special loads to transfer to the Down yard to connect with other evening Class C express freight departures. This heavy workload demanded a very high standard of shunting over the small, raised 'knuckle' and an impeccable understanding between the driver of the pilot engine, the head shunter, the man in the ground frame controlling the points and the wagon chasers who slowed down the shunted wagons.

There were very few mishaps at Whitemoor, less than two wagons damaged in each thousand shunted, but when an accident did occur it could be spectacular. On one notable occasion the Up yard was shunting a train from Doncaster when a bogie bolster wagon loaded with steel, having passed safely through No.1 retarder, came to a dead stop in No.2. Its load of steel failed to follow suit, headed forward and then nosedived into the ground. This reversed the direction of the 'Bobol' into the path of ten wooden coal wagons with an incredible heap of debris resulting from the meeting. Another similar occasion had a happier outcome when a steel wagon stopped while its load continued but was then restored to its original position when pushed forward again by the impact of the next wagon down.

Station Handbells

The practice of ringing a handbell five minutes before train departure time was widespread in the early railway years. Since they were the years when only a modest proportion of intending passengers owned yet alone carried a watch, some means was needed of alerting intending travellers to the need to join their train. At Lossiemouth, for example, the station bell was a godsend to the fishwives of the town. Many bought fish at the south end of the harbour, near to the station, packed it into creels and then carried their wares daily by train to Elgin for sale. The bell was valued not only by these ladies but was also useful for the intending passengers absorbed in taking refreshment in the bar of the Station Hotel.

This Lossiemouth station bell had a venerable history. It had started life in the turret of the castle home of the Gordons of Gordonstoun but then passed to the Lossiemouth harbourmaster who used it to herald the arrival and departure of vessels. When the trains arrived in 1852 they killed off the sailing ship service so the bell was passed over to the station and there mounted on the platform wall to begin a new period of usefulness by warning of train departures and marking the 10 a.m. railway time signal.

Station handbells continued in use at several London Tilbury & Southend line stations right into the 1950s. In 1952 the Westcliff-on-Sea bell was still being rung immediately before train departure and a bell was discovered at Southend Central and brought back into use. At the time Cromer Beach M&GN was still using its bell, believed to be of Eastern & Midlands Railway origin, and an ex-GNR bell remained at Yarmouth Beach, albeit out of use.

Conventional Booking Office

Until ticket printing and issuing machines were introduced railway booking offices had remained virtually unchanged for many years. On the main line between Hitchin and Huntingdon the one at Biggleswade was typically GNR, with a booking hall and an office with a ticket window, parcels counter and adjoining parcels room. A class IV chief clerk presided over two class V subordinates on 6 a.m. to 2 p.m. and 2 p.m. to 10 p.m. turns. He did the monthly returns and balance sheet, the others issued the tickets and did the daily cash balances.

A typical day started with a rush of people wanting Workmen's Returns to Hitchin, all at the last minute and all draining precious change from the 'float' in the bowls in the cash drawer. Hardly had they left when the carmen arrived to

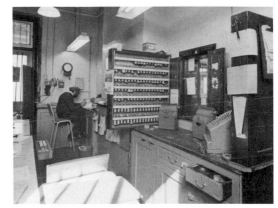

Machines are starting to appear in this SR booking office scene but the ticket rack, ticket window and cash drawer, together with the general clutter, remain typical of a generation of such offices.

collect their 'sheets', on which arriving parcels had been listed for delivery and signature. Next was the period before the departure of the morning fast service to King's Cross when tickets had to be 'flicked' from the racks, pushed in and out of the ferocious date press and then moved on through the ticket window, all in one fluid movement and accompanied by change that had already been placed in piles to match the most common transactions.

During the morning there were train and other enquiries to be dealt with and local people would drift in with parcels to be weighed and their 'face value' stamps or ledger labels fixed on with glue from a sticky, untidy pot. This was also the time for the daily balancing of the cash taken, with the debit represented by ticket issues, plus parcels, cloakroom and other such takings. In the case of printed stock the last number in each ticket tube, blank card book or other record was compared with the closing numbers for the previous day. Excess fares, dog, cycle and pram 'zones', 'privilege' tickets, 'firewood sales' and all the other odds and ends were embraced in the process with the fervent hope that the debits and credits would balance and life could resume its normal rhythm.

Less than normal events did occur from time to time, like the arrival of a man carrying a 10ft sailing dinghy mast and asking for a return ticket to London. Chief Clerk Harry told him that he 'could not travel with that thing' in a tone that the would-be passenger construed as less than helpful. Exasperated, he tried to poke the boat mast through the ticket window and impale Harry on it. Only a rush to lock the connecting door from the ticket hall saved the day. The same happened when Harry had another peevish day and responded to the offer of a large banknote for a ridiculously small fare with the remark, 'Do you think this is the Bank of England?'

In fairness it has to be said that Harry knew absolutely all there was to know about passenger traffic. Nothing foxed him: forces warrants, prisoner with escort journeys, commercial travellers' luggage, special rates for grooms and pigeon handlers and so on. He was a small, slight man who felt the cold in winter and never conceded an inch of his privileged position in front of the roaring office coal fire. Not even on the day we juniors determined to shift him by building it up to furnace proportions. We failed. Harry stayed put, even when the varnish on his chair began to bubble!

Unconventional Booking Office

A highly imaginative educational experiment returned booking facilities to Gobowen on the Shrewsbury–Chester line. Girls from Moreton Hall

This unconventional booking office on the North Somerset line was located in the Miners' Arms public house.

School undertook the staffing of an office in the old gatekeeper's cottage from 6.30 a.m. to 6 p.m., six days a week, and sold a full range of tickets there as a fully computerised BR travel agency.

Private Arrangements

Quite a few negotiations between early railways and landowners resulted in the latter demanding special facilities as a condition of selling their land. A favourite was stipulating the provision of a private station or special stopping arrangements. In one case, that of Corrour on the West Highland line, the private station was also a railway-manned signalling block post and crossing point.

One private station which appeared in the public timetables was Dunrobin (Private) on the Highland route north from Inverness to Wick. The Duke of Sutherland had made a major contribution to the building of this remote line and in return had the right, subject to notice and complying with train operating regulations, to run his own train over the route. The Duke's 1895 0-4-4T locomotive was used on 23 April 1938 to haul an LMS official saloon carrying the Prime Minister back from Dunrobin Castle on the first stage of his journey back to London.

Not all private arrangements worked out so well. There was a long-standing story that Devil's Bridge at Uphill in Somerset was named after a notoriously awkward Squire Payne who had driven the Bristol & Exeter Railway surveyors off his land because 'trains were dangerous and would set the country on fire'. Eventually access was agreed on the understanding that a station was built for Payne in the cutting near the bridge. However, when he came to request a train stop for a journey to London the B&E replied that it had only agreed to build a station, not to stop trains there!

Brunel told of a case where a man had erected a 'house' made of brown paper over a timber frame in order to claim compensation 'for having diminished the value of his property' when building a bridge embankment on the Oxford line. In contrast a man who was treated badly was a wealthy city gent who had retired to Tankerton and offered to provide the Southern Railway with up to £2,000 to build a simple station for the growing community there. The result was Chestfield & Swalecliffe Halt. Sadly, on his first visit, the man who put up the cash was made to buy a platform ticket.

In more recent years there have been quite a few cases of commercial firms funding a station for their employees' benefit, one such example being Acrow Halt near Saffron Walden.

Curious Cases

The railway system had several curious border and boundary situations. Knighton station, on a delightful section of the Central Wales Line, is in England but the town is in Wales, and when Kirkby Lonsdale station was open in the former county of Westmorland, the station for the town was actually located two miles inside Lancashire. Some stations even had platforms in different counties, such as Hay and Newmarket.

Yorkshire and Durham featured in a railway *quid pro quo* with Middleton-in-Teesdale village on the Durham side of the River Tees and its station in Yorkshire, while the reverse applied in the case of Yarm. This latter situation caused a slight complication in the cricketing world when Yorkshire discovered that the famous Cecil Parkin was not actually qualified by birth to play for the county since he had been born in the station house at Yarm. Lancashire was not so fussy.

Examples of stations that existed only for interchange purposes and had no external access included Bala Junction, Roudham Junction, Barnwell Junction and Methven and Cairnie Junctions in Scotland. South Molton Road was 9 miles from the town it served!

Dartmouth

Dartmouth had the distinction of being a station without trains, being served by the railway-owned ferry across the River Dart from Kingswear. The

The former Dartmouth station building is now a restaurant but still betrays its railway origins. From the quay behind the ferry crosses to Kingswear.

original Dartmouth & Torbay Railway had, at one stage, planned to cross the river higher up and run its trains down the west bank to Dartmouth itself, but the Bill for the alteration was defeated in the House of Lords due to opposition from the principal landowner

When the first section of the line was opened south to Paignton in 1859 the celebrations there included the cooking of a mammoth 2,100lb 'Paignton Pudding'. So great was the demand for a piece of this culinary giant that a gang of workmen charged the cart on which it was being carried and were only repelled when the servers pelted them with lumps of the steaming pudding.

Wemyss Bay

Quite a number of railway stations provided access to shipping vessels varying in size from small ferries to ocean liners. Their design varied, too, from the extended platform which provided access to the Humber paddle steamers at New Holland to the huge quayside stations at places like Parkeston Quay and Dover. As befitted their special status many of these stations had some claim to architectural 'style', among them Wemyss Bay where the elegant concourse still curves down to an ornate quayside building and the regular sailings to and from Rothesay.

The covered waiting area at Wemyss Bay used by passengers transferring from trains to the Caledonian MacBrayne steamers to and from the Isle of Bute.

Departmental Depots

The Signal & Telecommunications Engineer, the Chief Civil Engineer, the Motive Power people, the Road Motor engineers and so on all had their own depots. These housed the staff and materials to carry out countless support jobs like power supplies, water and lighting, weed killing and bridge painting.

An example of one of the less well-known depots was located at Lowestoft where the sleeper depot supplied the permanent way activity from its stock of over 200,000 wooden sleepers. The sleepers themselves were imported and stacked in the open to season before eventually being cut to size and drilled to accommodate chairs or baseplates. After passing through spiked rollers to assist creosote penetration they were loaded onto small trolleys and fed into the creosote cylinders where they were 'cooked' for around thirty-six hours. The chairs or baseplates were then bolted on and the sleepers loaded to wagons for despatch.

Stationmaster's View

In 1962 a stationmaster on a minor branch line responded to a request for information on the history of his station with the following words:

> Our business is normally placid and undisturbed and I can only recall the following incidents:-
>
> In March 1947 the line was washed away by floods just north of here, and for two days we had no service to Buntingford.
>
> During September 1953 a film company took possession of the station for a fortnight when filming 'Happy Ever After'. All station nameplates were altered to Rathbarney, and we were made to look like a small Irish station. The station was crowded with technicians, extras, cameramen, producers etc., and I'm sure Braughing station had never before seen so many people. About three years later 'Girls in Arms' was also partly filmed here.
>
> The last time the branch was blocked was in February 1958 when snow drifts resulted in the 5pm train from Buntingford, with about fifty passengers aboard, being snowed up between Standon and Hadham. We had a light engine here and it was decided to use it to try to push the stranded train through to Hadham.
>
> We managed to get just beyond Standon when we ran into deep drifts and could not move in either direction. I was carrying the train staff and started to walk the three miles to Hadham. A gale was blowing, it was dark and I could

not keep my handlamp alight. The snow was up to my waist in places and my Wellington boots were full of melted snow.

At last I found the disabled train which by now looked almost completely covered in snow. I advised the passengers and crew of the position and continued my exhausting walk, sometimes on the track and sometimes over the fields. I was jolly glad finally to arrive at Hadham and receive a good, stiff brandy from the station master there. Guard Hills from Buntingford had walked from the disabled train to Hadham. He was so exhausted that he had to have medical attention.

Wells-on-Sea

The small town of Wells on the north Norfolk coast got its first trains in 1857 when the Wells & Fakenham Railway opened. Soon afterwards branches were opened to the harbour and west along the coast to Heacham. For over a century the railway served its community well and also carried thousands of pilgrims to the Roman Catholic shrine near Walsingham. Today the town has a new name, Wells-next-the-Sea, and the main line railway has been replaced by two narrow-gauge tourist lines, one south along the trackbed of the original 1857 line and the other running beside the tidal channel to the sea.

Personal memories of Wells-on-Sea, as it then was, include dealing with the countless small, wet and smelly bags of cockles forwarded by passenger train. Each bag had a label but getting a parcels stamp to adhere to the damp reverse was an acquired skill. Like most GE section stations the single-needle telegraph instrument at Wells was located in the booking office. It was not easy to use at the best of times but the circuit from Heacham was liable to be affected by weather extremes causing the needle to chatter away in its own completely mystifying gibberish. Needless to say newcomers were not warned of this situation until near-demented with trying to decipher the undecipherable.

TWELVE

JOBS AND PEOPLE

Nothing highlights more the rich variety of the railway activity than an insight into the jobs railwaymen performed and the sort of people who performed them. The earliest recruits had only modest skills and absolutely no experience or precedents. Some came from the coaching activity that the railways displaced, some from the ranks of the engineers who had built the lines and the rest from every conceivable walk of life.

They learned quickly and well and produced an ongoing corps of railwaymen proud of their professional skills and dedicated to supplying safe and efficient transport. Needless to say the railway jobs and people were as varied as other aspects of rail transport.

The Teemers

One of the very earliest of railway activities was the movement of coal over primitive wagonways to the north-east coast for shipment. For years railway staff performed the loading and trimming of colliers, over seventy teemers being employed at West Blyth in the post-war years. When the last BR timber-decked gravity loading staithes there closed in the 1960s the loading process was still in the hands of these railway teemers, graded as senior railmen but working to their own special job rules and conditions. Operating in gangs of four the teemers were paid on a 'keelage' basis which derived from the era of the old keel boats and their normal load of 21.5 tons.

The teemers were not only skilled in their job but had a good eye for the various types of coal arriving by wagon from the north-east collieries. As one observed, 'We got the best money for loading pond duff, washed small and slack, which had the consistency of wet cement!' Widdrington opencast was 'free flowing' and Shilbottle Best a firm favourite because it was mined from between two layers of white pyrites, giving the lumps a white coating.

This is not to say that teemers were all angels, for trows and ketches working out of the railway docks at Newport in South Wales used to dread being loaded on the last shift of the day when there was a tendency to drop a whole wagon load down the shute without restraint and to cover the ship's crew with a huge cloud of black coal dust in the process.

A 1925 GWR Vanguard

The vanguard needed to be a hardy character to ride on the back of an open vehicle in all weathers, or in a cab with no windscreen. He needed to be strong enough to hump 2.25cwt sacks of grain or 2cwt hessian sacks of cement with rock-like deposits to tear at one's fingers. Frozen quarters of beef were carried high on the shoulder where they flattened and froze the ears. He might have to shovel sugar beet throughout a pouring wet day, with rain running out of his pants into squelching wet boots.

The vehicles on which I learned to drive were ex-First World War AEC lorries capable of 12mph flat out and with solid tyres, 'gate' gearboxes, and a man-sized starting handle to swing fifty times a day. The vanguard had to crawl under the rear end to grease the differential each morning. He also had to polish the brass oil side lights which, on a good night, were just capable of illuminating the alloy radiator! Another part of the job was to look in the shop windows we passed to see if the rear light still burned!

Among the scary moments was careering downhill for 3 miles with a faulty trailer brake and a 5-ton load of grain on the lorry and another 5 tons on the trailer, and then shooting the lot into the road on the sharp bend at the bottom!

In these words Ray Manners describes his first experiences after joining the GWR as a vanguard at Bath depot in 1925. Over a forty-six-year career he worked his way up from this lowly start to a senior position with Freightliners Ltd via such varied posts as summer relief cloakroom attendant at Weymouth and cartage supervisor at Swindon. His induction into the infant world of road transport was informal and began with 'unofficial and surreptitious movements in the goods yard'. Then came the memorable day on the road to collect a load of Harbutt's plasticine when his driver put Ray's hands on the steering wheel and invited him to 'slide his backside' over the 30-gallon fuel tank into the driving position – all with out slowing down or getting the wagon out of gear!

Invoices and Waybills

One of the most taxing clerical jobs was the preparation of documents to go
with urgent and perishable traffic, despatched in quantity and with very little
time between arrival at the station and the departure time of the forward
service. One example was the forwarding of fish catches from Yarmouth
and Lowestoft during the East Anglian Herring Season. As the herring
shoals moved south the trawlers and drifters from further up the East Coast
joined the local boats and discharged their catches at local ports for onward
movement by rail to Billingsgate and other markets.

At Lowestoft the fish were unloaded, sold and packed at the Fish Dock
and then carted to the sidings beside the Inner Harbour. While the fish vans
were being loaded there, the office staff frantically wrote out waybills for
each fish consignment so that they would be ready to go beneath the wagon
labels when the Class C fitted express train services departed. Extra seasonal
staff were drafted in for this job, a few weeks of which played havoc with the
author's handwriting. However, there were compensations in the memories
of the fishing boats returning to port, the hectic fish market scenes, the fisher
girls gutting fish at their stalls and in the grand taste of fish which reached
one's table so quickly after being caught.

Two of the Wisbech tramway engines at Cambridge locomotive depot in the 1950s.

A similar situation arose during the Cambridgeshire Fruit Season and on the Wisbech & Upwell Tramway this was tackled by using one van as an office van. On the first morning service out from Wisbech a clerk was dropped off at each station along the route, with two going through to the end of the line at Upwell. At peak periods enough fruit was brought into the wayside depots to make up six daily trains of vans for hauling back to Wisbech. The staff had to prepare the waybills at a furious pace while the loading was taking place and then continue the process on the journey in with the office van.

Many other such movements put railway staff on their mettle. One was the Salvation Army's *War Cry* when it was despatched from the printers at St Albans. Another was the forwarding of Huntley & Palmer's biscuits from Reading. In the days before supermarkets these went to hundreds of different local grocers and each consignment had to be accompanied by an invoice. The task was made harder by the fact that the biscuits were loose-packed in tins, varied in weight and sold to the trade at so much per hundredweight. In addition, the tins were returnable against a deposit!

Air-Raid Warnings

At the outbreak of war sixteen-year-old Fernley Maker had the task of passing on the air-raid warnings received at Plymouth. At the time main railway offices had a GPO telephone but internal railway communications relied on local 'omnibus' circuits where the recipient was summoned by a bell code. The railway received its warnings before the local sirens were sounded and when an 'Air Raid Warning Yellow' was received on Plymouth 5069, the booking office telephone, young Fernley had to run round to the inspectors' office and hold down the key on each of the two circuits there for thirty seconds. For a 'Red' alert the code was four short rings repeated four times, and for 'All Clear' the signal was two short and two long rings sent three times. Devonport signal box sent the message forward on the Tavistock circuit and Bere Alston alerted those on the Callington circuit.

Assorted Characters

In the 1960s Moreton-in-Marsh was still a rather 'feudal' station steeped in the timeless GWR order of things. There was a lot of first class travel to and from the station and the staff were adept at looking after this prime source of gratuities – 'weaseling' it would have been called in London. Harry, one of the station foremen, was the best judge of a tip prospect and would be first to open the arriving commuter's car door just as soon as it came to rest in the car park. Harry was an inveterate smoker and always had a cigarette secreted in the palm of his hand where, over the years, he had developed a large patch of dark, smoke-stained palm.

Wesley also worked at Moreton-in-Marsh. He was the goods clerk but had a desk in the booking office where he covered the duties between the early and late turn booking clerks. Wesley wore a long raincoat and a trilby hat green with age and never removed his cycle clips, either indoors or out. He was a stalwart of the local church choir and was popularly believed to keep the clips on even when wearing his cassock.

My own period in charge of the Cartage & Terminals section of the suburban district goods manager's office at Gordon Hill brought me in contact with several admirable characters. The sheer professionalism of the small team who drove relief motors and cranes was incredible. With the help of Inspectors Hayden and MacPhee they could and did handle anything. The routine work involved matching resources to traffic, sorting out problems and keeping a watch on results. The non-routine was immensely varied. We dealt with a lot of out-of-gauge loads needing special wagons, careful loading and securing and the arranging of a route that would accommodate their abnormal dimensions. Getting show traffic onto the showground was another non-routine and challenging task, especially as some of the exhibits were on a strict show-to-show timetable. Memories include managing to deliver 60ft long rails on a 6-ton Bedford articulated unit and trailer by using ballast blocks on the tractor and a homemade support gantry on the trailer. And in the ASLE&F strike of 1955 one of the relief drivers, Vic Groves I think, took an urgent load from London to Edinburgh in a 3-ton Scammell mechanical horse and trailer; all that way with a 3-wheeled motor unit!

The chief of the General Section was Cyril, a very pleasant and experienced man. His idiosyncrasy was filling his petrol lighter with railway fuel, no great crime but it made the lighter smoke badly so that after lighting a few cigarettes Cyril invariably had a black smudge extending up from the bridge of his nose to his hair line.

The Inspector Class

Fairly recently a very senior railwayman deplored the loss of the old railway 'inspector' class. He likened them to the warrant officers, petty officers and senior NCOs of the armed forces. Such men did, indeed, make a major contribution to railway operation and efficiency and possessed great qualities of knowledge, experience and enterprise. The author's Traffic

Apprentice training included a period with the March-based district inspector and odd days out with the chief inspector from Cambridge. They taught me a lot about practical railway work and also how to compensate for the bad times, occasions like dealing with accidents, sorting out traffic problems on dark cold nights and the other such stressful tasks, with an occasional bit of self-indulgence.

After so many years I cannot remember why we were out in the Fens at Shippea Hill on the Ely–Norwich line, a lonely place in the middle of a flat, fertile and sparsely inhabited landscape. It was never much of a station and the adjacent pub looked much as it had done when the navvies who built the line had used it. Since we did not get to the pub until nearly two o'clock I was resigned to another day without any lunch. Wrong; less than an hour after our arrival a door to the private quarters of this tiny, ancient pub opened and a large matronly lady beckoned us through to reveal a table immaculately laid and a meal that matched any the Great Eastern Hotel could have served up. It was clearly not the first time this had happened but I enquired no further.

Unconventional Solution

At one period in 1969, Gloucester – the old Midland station – was overwhelmed with parcels for transhipment. Peter Nicholls was sent there with a remit to help Area Manager Bob Poynter sort the matter out – '48 hours should do it', the divisional movements manager had said – and found the platforms knee deep in unsorted parcels and with trains from Birmingham, Nottingham and so on still waiting to be unloaded. The cause of the trouble was that loaded vans were arriving with traffic for destinations in the south and west with their contents completely unsorted.

Every solution was tried, working overtime, taking on more staff, streamlining the sorting process, but the station stood no chance while the root cause of the problem remained unaltered. With representations through normal channels having no effect only drastic action would achieve improvement, so Bob Poynter got a light engine off the shed, found a crew who knew the road as far as Barnt Green and sent the next unsorted train back where it had come from. Birmingham Control was furious, the LM Region was furious and general managers got involved, but the end result was a break to clear up the arrears and better sorting of subsequent arrivals.

Harold Tippler

Harold Tippler was born in 1880 and began his association with railways at Spalding at the age of fourteen when he got a job as a bookstall boy for W.H. Smith Ltd. He remembered selling travelling rugs, Bradshaw timetables and short thick candles for those who wanted to read in the dark carriages of the time. Three years later Harold joined the GNR as the stationmaster's messenger boy and found that two of his relief signalmen colleagues had joined as 'bobbies'. His memories after ninety years still included the era of footwarmers, rape oil roof lamps and the construction of the Bourne-Saxby line.

Among the other things Harold mentioned in a letter to the author was the external communication cord system. He described how the cord ran along the roof edge of each coach to loops at the end and was then linked by hook to the cord of the next vehicle. To signal an emergency the passenger would have to open the carriage window, reach up and pull the cord downwards. In the guard's van a pivoted metal arm struck a bell and, hopefully, led to an application of the brake.

Group Training

Quite as interesting as people performing their normal jobs is the observation of people undergoing training. The interest seemed to be heightened in the case of management training where the participants often had quite distinctive personal qualities, usually including a highly developed sense of humour.

The pressure of being observed did not make for relaxation or normality, a fact I first realised on a course where very senior people joined us for breakfast. My knife somehow got balanced on the edge of the table and when my elbow caught it and set it off on a wild somersault across the staid dining room where everyone appeared to stop talking to marvel at my feat. I was then confirmed in the feeling that it was not my day when I helpfully passed a very august personage the sugar bowl and watched in dismay as the tongues fell off and plummeted into a milk jug with a resounding splash.

Memories of the senior management course at Woking are happier ones. There were thirty-four of us, including a Belgian, a Canadian and a major from the Royal Corps of Transport. The teaching input was rich, intense and varied – effective speaking, critical path analysis, seminars, practical exercises and so on – but well leavened by a few extra-curricular activities. On a routine day these might comprise a late and noisy game of

Traditionally the eight weeks of intense study involved in a BR senior management course was followed by end-of-course entertainment provided by the students. The sketch shown parodied the assessment process by assessing the tutorial staff themselves.

liar dice or the earnest efforts of the barbershop quartet that the Canadian member felt obliged to tutor. On the trip to Europe a tour of Schipol Airport was followed by a sing-song on an Amsterdam tram that was so well received we were requested to continue and did several circuits of the route, hardly pausing between numbers. Mind you, the gaunt, pallid group that disembarked at Parkeston Quay at the end of the three days in Europe looked anything but top-quality managers.

By tradition each Woking Course put on an 'entertainment' at the end of the eight weeks of study and our No.16 Course embraced the idea with enthusiasm. The result was a variety show which featured countless popular tunes with rewritten, often scurrilous, lyrics and several highly imaginative sketches. Two that stick in my mind are the performance of the 'girls' of the 'Woking Ladies' Finishing School' and a sketch entitled 'The Appraisals'. Mercilessly this aped the process of our evaluation and reporting back to our regions but substituted appraisals of the course tutors and other personnel which only just avoided being libellous.

THIRTEEN

CONTROL

Railways have always planned their operations – train timetables, locomotive and stock movements, staff rosters, operational and traffic handling practices – well in advance. There were countless books of instruction, such as the universal Rule Book issued to all staff, General and Sectional Appendices for operating staff and the Coaching Arrangements Book for booking clerks. One-off activities were usually covered by a special notice, a practice much used before modern communications. Later the telegraph network and modern telephone systems steadily closed the time gap between arranging an event and its execution.

From the 1920s until the first electrical relay systems and panel signal boxes began to emerge the efficient day-to-day running of the railway system depended on the traffic control offices located at major centres. Under a deputy chief controller, each of the three eight-hour shifts had its section controllers covering individual sections of line and other desks devoted to controlling locomotives and rolling stock, dealing with special traffics and keeping the performance records which would provide the basis for righting faults and shortcomings. There were many similarities to standard air traffic control arrangements.

Great Western Railway

Way back in 1883 the GWR's Superintendent of the Line at Paddington issued Notice No. 57 on 23 April regarding a Broad Gauge Special Train that was to be run for 'the conveyance of Lord Falmouth's Servants, Horses and Carriages' from Truro to London. The text indicated that the train would consist of four horse boxes, six carriage trucks, one saloon, a second class coach and a 'luggage van with break'. It was booked to leave Truro at 6 p.m. on 25 April and arrive in London at 4.50 a.m. the following morning.

This was good business for the Great Western and as a patron of some importance was involved the notice stated 'It is very important that this Train should be worked to time', and added 'Station Masters must see that all Goods, Mineral and Cattle Trains are shunted and kept clear of the above Train'. The guard had to be given a supply of report forms and use them to report on the execution of the journey to local officials and to the Superintendent of the Line himself. Woe betided any signalman or shunter who delayed such a train.

BR(WR) West of England Division, 17 January 1968

This was just a typical day in the Control Office in the former Bristol & Exeter Railway headquarters building at Bristol. It started with a derailment at Frome and a signalling block failure between Gillingham and Wilton caused by the theft of copper wire. Many of the thirty-one log entries over the twenty-four hours from 6.00 a.m. were routine items covering engine and equipment failures, special traffic arrangements and the like but one or two reflected the rich variety that traffic controllers regularly encountered on their shifts.

17.04 Pilning Inspector reported that the 16.05 Severn Tunnel–Acton which came in the tunnel STW [Severn Tunnel West] 16.42 and arrived STE at 16.57 requested to be looped owing to engine difficulties. Failed at entrance to loop at 17.00. D839 load 35, Severn Tunnel men. D1750 en route from Stoke Gifford to Bath Road shed intercepted at Filton and sent to Pilning at 17.12. Arrived at Pilning 17.24 and left with WLO [Wrong Line Order] to get onto train and pull in clear at 17.47.

15.20 Swansea–Paddington delayed STW and came in 17.48, 50 late.

16.35 Cardiff–Bristol STW 54 late

16.45 Cardiff–Portsmouth STW 52 late

00.25 Plymouth advise that Devon & Cornwall Police had advised them at 00.20 that an unidentified caller had phoned the Western Morning News that 'the Tamar Bridge would not be there in the morning.' Plymouth Police advised, also DM [Divisional Manager], AM [Area Manager], DI [District Inspector] and adjacent signal boxes. Civil police have matter in hand.

00.25 Plymouth advise 18.30 Paddington–Penzance delayed at Newton Abbot 22.32–22.50 after striking two rear Brutes [parcels trolleys] out of six empty Brutes which were being towed over barrow crossing from Up to Down side. Mr Bath called out and attempts being made to push Brutes clear with a Scott tractor. Two Brutes are a write off. Train engine D1058 (84A) damaged and replaced by D864.

Interestingly the Passenger Train Punctuality sheet for the day showed that of 192 trains 114 arrived on time but only seventy-four left on time, something the chief controller would doubtless be pursuing. Another forty were one to two minutes late arriving.

BR(ER) Kings Cross Division, 5 March 1967

It was a Sunday and the weather was logged as fine as the DCC took duty at 8 a.m. There was nothing out of the ordinary on the first shift and the second one started off well enough; just a locomotive boiler defect, a water seepage at King's Cross station, a Cambridge diesel multiple unit over-running the platform at Finsbury Park and delay to the 17.46 from Grimsby at Peterborough. Then it all went wrong and the log recorded:

> 1A72 22.30 Kings Cross to Edinburgh derailed between Connington South and Connington North – at 23.40 Grantham Guard Wright reported to the No.3 Section Controller that the train was derailed and vehicles on their sides. 1A72 passed Connington South 23.36. Peterborough Civil Police advised 23.42, Huntingdon Constabulary 23.45 and requested to send ambulance, doctors and fire brigade.

The Flying Scotsman on the East Coast Main Line near Huntingdon.

BT police and divisional officers advised. New England and Kings Cross B.D. [breakdown] vans ordered 23.45. 6 bells ['Obstruction Danger'] sent Connington South to Abbots Ripton 23.39.

At 23.54 Guard Wright reported from Connington South that the 4 rear coaches were derailed and on their sides. Several passengers killed and under vehicles. Wright stated he had no lights and required assistance quickly. Derailed vehicles about 200 yards north of Connington South box. Kings Cross Driver Oakton, Fireman Wheaton, locomotive D9004. BD vans depart New England 00.51, Kings Cross 01.10.

At 01.10 District Inspector Keys reported from Connington South that the train was divided engine and 7 vehicles on first portion. Seventh vehicle was derailed north end and leaning towards the Down Goods line. The 8th, 9th, 10th, 11th vehicles had been severed from their bogies and were on their sides and on their roof – leaning towards the Down Goods line. Up Main blocked in two places by debris and bogies. Front portion consists mainly of GPO vans. Police had ordered a bus to convey passengers to Peterborough. Arrangements made to run a Special from Peterborough. Mr Young at Peterborough asked to arrange to provide refreshments and accommodation at the GN Hotel. Provisional figures 6 dead, 5 injured.

Formation of train from the engine – BG 81342, POS 70293, POS 70296, POT 70298, SLF 2414, SK24210, SK 25860 – parting – SK 24034, CK 16243, BSK 3416, BG 81206. Engine and first vehicles off 1A72 left Connington North 02.08, arrived Peterborough 02.21 and terminated. After CW (Carriage & Wagon) examination there vehicles were attached to the front of 1A04

Huntingdon Police reported at 02.05 that 6 people had been killed and 10 injured but not seriously. Names obtained of injured who had all been taken to Peterborough Memorial Hospital – 9 released, 8 detained.

When the derailment occurred 1NO1 22.45 Kings Cross to Leeds/Bradford was approaching Abbots Ripton. The train was stopped at Abbots Ripton IBH [signal] at 23.43 and arrangements made to draw the train back to Huntingdon and re-route via Hitchin and Cambridge. D5594 left Hitchin 00.23, arrived Abbots Ripton 01.00, on train 01.06. 1NO1 left the IBH 01.23 with WLO [Wrong Line Order] to Huntingdon where the train was crossed to the Up Main line and arrived Hitchin 02.16, dep 02.23 via Cambridge.

> Permanent Way Damaged – Mr Rodgers Area Assistant, Peterborough reported from Connington the Down Main had been extensively damaged for a distance of about 600 yards.

Subsequent entries covered the resulting passenger train cancellations and diversions, the special bus service laid on between Huntingdon and Peterborough, the revision of freight services, the provision of food for staff working at Connington and so on.

This was a tragic event and the log only hints at the agony and drama of the mishap and the incredible efforts of the railway staff and those of the emergency services involved in this derailment. Matters were not helped by the fact that it occurred in the middle of the night and that the Connington Heath site was not the easiest to reach by road. Despite it functional language the control log does, however, reveal something of the professionalism of the railwaymen involved, both at the scene and in the support locations.

FOURTEEN

TRACTION

Since the romance of railways found its best expression in the locomotive it is hardly surprising that motive power and footplate anecdotes abound. The first locomotives excited sheer wonder while later designers and builders took so many different directions that each class tended to have its own peculiar features. There were different combinations of leading, driving and trailing wheels, differing valve gears, variations in boiler pressure and steam supply and other design differences on each railway, while experimentation with things like oil burning, compounding and streamlining further expanded the number of locomotive types. Some were built for high track adhesion, some for sheer pulling power and others for the dividends deriving from high speed. Each class had its fans and most enjoyed an affectionate nickname, be it Cauliflowers, Buckjumpers or Jinties.

Back to its Routes

One of the locomotive exhibits at the Manchester Museum of Science and Industry caused massive delays to commuters on services from Bolton and Liverpool when it made a bid for freedom in June 1996. The exhibit was a replica of the 1830 Liverpool & Manchester Railway locomotive *Planet* housed in the museum established at the former L&M station at Manchester, Liverpool Road.

Gathering momentum from its rail site just inside the museum *Planet* crashed through the boundary gate and derailed itself just short of the main line, breaking both its axles in the process. It was almost as if the old engine was bent on returning to its original line. Fortunately inspection revealed that there was just sufficient clearance to permit the modern trains to pass but it was a week before the runaway could be recovered and restored to its proper home.

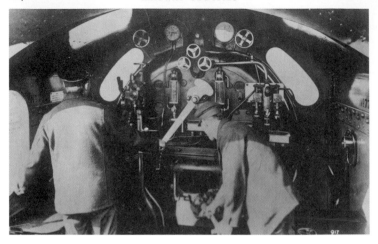

A view of a steam locomotive footplate and the crew's controls.

Model Record

On 23 March 1990 the duration record for model locomotives was challenged. The previous 864-hour 30-minute record held by a Hornby 'Britannia' was put to the test by Hornby models of an HST, *Evening Star*, *King Richard I* and *Lady Patricia*. During the thirty-six-day marathon the first three succumbed to electrical brush failure leaving the oo-gauge 'Princess Royal' class model the winner with a new record of 867 hours 14 minutes.

Driving Contracts

However strange it may seem now it was, at one time, not unusual for locomotive drivers to operate under contracts which paid them an agreed sum for each mile run and left them to pay the costs of achieving this. The practice dates back at least to 1830 when the Stockton & Darlington Railway paid its drivers a farthing for each ton mile of haulage.

On some lines such contract payments to drivers were still in use thirty years later, the payment rate varying with the type of work undertaken. Out of his remuneration the driver had to pay his fireman and engine cleaner, purchase coal or coke and other consumables and also meet the bill for some replacements and repairs such as brake blocks and similar items affected by his driving skills. He got charged if his engine needed assistance or ran badly late but received extra cash for assisting other train engines when needed.

The system was clearly designed to encourage good timekeeping and economical running and when things went well a driver could do quite well out of his contract.

One drawback was the risk of drivers trying to conserve steam by pinning down their safety valves, a factor which appeared to be behind the explosion of a Manchester & Leeds Railway locomotive in Miles Platting engine shed in 1845 when three people were killed and the roof blown off the building.

Ill-Fated Locomotive

Class 40 locomotive No.40126 is a strong contender for being BR's most jinxed locomotive. It hit the headlines as the engine of the Glasgow–London postal train robbed of £2.6 million but had previously been involved in a collision near Crewe in which eighteen people died and thirty-three were injured. There were other unhappy events in this locomotive's career, too, with a fitter working on its roof being electrocuted and a guard being injured when 40126 ran away on the approach to Birmingham New Street station.

Footplate Tyros

The traditional training programme for railway 'Traffic Apprentices' included several months with the motive power department in steam sheds, traction depots, main works and headquarters offices. They had to grapple with the system of footplate links and promotion, the manning rosters, engine records, availability and allocation, the repair and shopping systems and the great variety of jobs on and around the shed. All had to be understood, from the work of the Running Shed Foreman to that of the steam raisers, fire droppers and sand furnace attendants. Finally, after a period of wholly strange and uncomfortable tasks like testing the firebox stays and building a brick arch, came the thrill of a week on the footplate.

As part of his period at March Loco, the author's first footplate trip was with B17 Class No.61643 *Champion Lodge*. In the hands of Driver Wakeling and Fireman Burgess the 4-6-0 took over the afternoon Newcastle–Lowestoft passenger train from March to Norwich and then worked back with the 7.38 p.m. Class D goods from Crown Point.

The B17 on the next day, No.61619 *Welbeck Abbey*, provided an entirely different experience. Just out of shops, she was pretty stiff, and with a heavy load and tight timings both ways Driver Ward and Fireman Ellington had a hard day. The run through Clarborough Tunnel was memorable for my first such experience of smoke blowing back, the noise reverberating at a deafening level off the walls and the open firebox door casting a fiery orange glow over our tiny space on the footplate.

Day 3 and Diagram 13 meant taking the Lowestoft–Newcastle in the opposite direction, this time at 9.54 a.m. from March and 2.50 p.m. back from York. Driver Head and Fireman Robinson were allocated V2 Class locomotive No.60803 and I joined them on the prepared engine and with great anticipation for I had loved the look of this class ever since my early days on the LNER. I got my opportunity with the shovel on the flat Lincolnshire stretch, trying to heed the fireman's kindly advice to 'put the coal where the fire is burning brightest'. Now the V2 was a princess among locomotives, strong, good looking and riding well thanks to the driving wheels being well forward of the cab, but in response to the kindly enquiry as to how I was doing honestly compelled the reply, 'Great, but if I can keep my feet and hit that ludicrously small hole in the firebox I'm quite pleased, never mind where the coal goes when I get it in there.' I got a tolerant smile and eventually learned better!

At York a Geordie driver took over for the onward leg to Newcastle. I listened to the changeover dialogue he had with my East Anglian driver and understood not a word. I'm not entirely sure they did either!

Journeys later in the week included a plod to Pywipe with O1 Class No.63875 hauling a Class F goods and an unscheduled changeover there to K3 No.61887 and a Class C special. The K3 was very rough, steaming badly and wasting water all the way but it made an interesting comparison with the earlier prestige passenger jobs. The final day's outing was to Bury St Edmunds and back with B1 Class engine No.61360 hauling light goods loads which she handled well despite injector trouble on the outward journey and a hot big end on the return.

Fellow Traffic Apprentice Trevor Anderson used to brag that one of his footplate trips had earned him a bonus. The crew he was with had worked a London–Paignton out and home turn with an Old Oak Common locomotive but slipped off to get a cup of tea when they got back into Paddington, leaving Trevor in charge. No sooner had they gone than Superintendent of the Line Gilbert Matthews emerged from the stream of detraining passengers, slipped 5s into Trevor's hand and remarked, 'Excellent trip, young man.' In an interview later in his career Trevor was able to remind the eminent man of the incident.

During his footplate period, Bill Bradshaw travelled on the 3 p.m. Capitals United Express from Cardiff to Paddington which was the back working of an Old Oak Common lodging turn who had taken the 5.55 p.m. Red Dragon down to Swansea the previous evening. The booked fireman had failed to turn up for duty and the OOC foreman had been forced to use in his place a young man who had not been out on the main line before. Fortunately the driver was a very calm and experienced man; the locomotive was in fine form and its coal the very best.

At Cardiff the Up train had been joined by a VIP party but the run through the Severn Tunnel and on to Stoke Gifford proceeded without hitch, Bill taking his turn with the shovel and the engine keeping to its tight schedule. Water was needed from the Chipping Sodbury troughs and the fireman duly lowered the scoop but Bill had seen before the need to wind it up at just the right time. On this occasion his inexperienced companion waited until the float indicator showed the tender full before starting to wind with the result that the cap, through which the tender was normally supplied from a static water crane, shot open and a huge fountain of water shot into the air. This was followed by a stream of coal and dust washed back down from the tender and swilling onto the footplate and crew. Although his mate got extremely dirty the driver had just calmly lifted his feet clear of the floor and sped on to achieve an arrival at Paddington seven minutes early but with the chocolate and cream coaches of the train overlaid with dirty streams of coal dust.

Anti-Vandal Patrols

British Transport Police have used radio-equipped light locomotives in the on-going fight against trespass and vandalism in both south Wales and Glasgow. In the Scottish experiment in 1976 over 250 arrests were made in the first four months of operation. The officers on the footplate were in constant radio contact with two unmarked cars supporting their efforts to apprehend suspects who were then taken back to the locomotive for identification and arrest.

Door Stop

During the Second World War brand new constable Bill Potts was patrolling along Barrow Road, Bristol, towards the bridge that spanned the LMS station, depot and sheds. He had been instructed to keep an eye open for pilfering from the depot and, being new, was doubly keen to make an arrest. Sad to say, pilfering was a fairly common wartime problem and 'winning' coal from railway depots was almost a legitimate practice, so long had it been going on. It was certainly more acceptable than the gang thefts of cigarettes and other goods for the black market from places like Nottingham.

However, theft was theft, and the young constable was fully alert as he approached the steps and gate that connected the bridge with the depot below. He could hardly believe his good fortune when his arrival there coincided with the emergence of a driver and fireman struggling to carry a huge lump of coal. Bill stepped into view and opened his mouth to caution the pair just as the quick-witted driver nodded towards the open gate, lowered his load and said to his companion, 'There we are, mate; this should stop the bloody thing from banging!'

Other Uses

Not a few locomotives have been used for things other than conventional train haulage. In Scotland, for example, the Provanhall Coal Co. used an 0-4-0T locomotive for hauling wagons up an incline by the unusual method of positioning it against buffer stops and over a winding drum which was turned by direct friction with the locomotive driving wheels.

Another Scottish enterprise was an early experiment with using a locomotive to tow vessels on the Forth & Clyde Canal. A special test track was laid beside the canal and the four-coupled locomotive *Victoria* borrowed from the Monkland & Kirkintilloch Railway ready for tests in August 1839. With two horses the normal Edinburgh to Glasgow passenger boats on the canal could achieve about 9mph but, according to reports of the locomotive test, '*Victoria* briskly set off and almost immediately gained a speed of 17.3mph'. The 'delighted passengers' were, apparently, 'highly gratified with the motion' but there the matter ended, probably due to the effect such boat speeds would have had on the canal banks.

Rainhill

That most exciting of events, the Rainhill Trials, conducted to find the best locomotion for the 1830 Liverpool & Manchester Railway, was dominated by the competition between *Rocket*, *Novelty* and *Sans Pareil*. But credit for interest, at least, must be given to the less serious entrants. The *Liverpool Courier* of 1829 recorded that Mr Brandreth's horse locomotive also showed its paces:

> ... not in the way of competition, but as exercise. About fifty persons clung round the waggons, giving a gross rate with the machine of about five tons, and with this weight the horses (themselves moving scarcely one mile and

a quarter an hour) propelled the wagons and load exactly at the rate of five miles an hour.

Another report records of Wednesday 14 October:

During the day there was also a demonstration of a 'manumotive' carriage invented by Winans, which was propelled by two men, and took six passengers. We are informed that it moved <u>with no great velocity.</u>

Extremes of Power

Away from the glamour of high-speed streamlined trains railways had a host of other motive power needs and private locomotive manufacturers responded with special designs for special jobs. The firm Wickhams of Ware, for example, produced a range of light motorised vehicles for carrying men and materials for track maintenance work. At the other extreme Beyer Peacock & Co. built huge articulated locomotives at their Manchester works

One of the many designs of Wickham trolley used by permanent way staff.

No.7973, one of the powerful Beyer Peacock locomotives purchased by the LMS for hauling long coal trains, is pictured at Crewe West in 1938.

This French pneumatic-tyred railcar stands at Cambridge during a trial period on the route to Bletchley and Oxford.

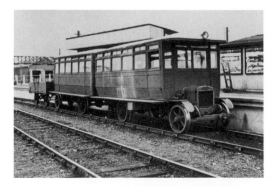

This curious Shefflex unit represents one of the earliest of many attempts to use bus construction technology to produce low cost trains for lightly trafficked routes.

for railways all over the world. The LMS took a number of these between 1928 and 1930 to handle its heavy coal trains.

The Search for Economy

With the growth of road transport railways paid increasing attention to reducing the costs of working lightly used rural lines. Steam and diesel railcars were numerous, with the search for the perfect design leading to several experiments with new types on the Bletchley to Cambridge line, including a French railcar fitted with pneumatic tyres.

Lickey Banker

Sometime in the mid-1950s Roger Lacy was working nights as Midland Control's outbased controller at Bromsgrove. The signalman at Bromsgrove South drew his attention to a departing bank engine as it set of to assist an Up freight train. 'Watch when he comes back,' said the signalman. Half an hour or so later the banker was back, worked just by the driver who shouted, 'Bobby, let us go up again as soon as you can.' Now this was highly unusual for the banking crews would normally do anything they could to minimise the number of runs they had to do.

Anyway, another train requiring assistance soon arrived and off went the driver, doing both the driving and firing jobs. When he got back the firemen was with him again and was carrying three lovely fish poached from the pool on the Up side of the bank. The crew had one each and handed over the third to the signalman for his co-operation.

Steaming Well

One summer Sunday around the same time Roger Lacy was again relieving as controller at Bromsgrove when a Saltley crew arrived at 5 a.m. with a Down freight, uncoupled to draw forward and took water in anticipation of continuing their journey. However, Roger had other ideas; they were to work back to Birmingham and leave their train to the Gloucester men who were just finishing their breakfast. The latter's guard called 'Ready when you are' as he walked to his brake, the driver and his mate climbed onto the footplate, checked the signal, whistled and set off. The signalman at Stoke Works was using the toilet when they passed and they got as far as Abbotswood before someone realised they had failed to couple to their train and were running 'light engine'. The driver's only comment when he returned was, 'I thought she was steaming well!'

Undercharge

Hugh Jenkins, later to become deputy general manager of the London Midland Region, had an early, but illicit, footplate trip on that region. At the time he was doing his Traffic Apprentice motive power training on the WR at Cardiff Canton depot and was issued with a footplate pass endorsed 'All Routes, Western Region'.

Deciding that a bit of inter-regional experience might be a good idea he presented himself to the driver of the Stanier Pacific *City of Coventry* about to haul the Mid-Day Scot out of Euston on a day in 1959. By keeping his thumb on the 'Western Region' limitation on his pass he got his trip and was allowed to fire the locomotive during the journey to Glasgow.

After an exhilarating but exhausting run Hugh started his return journey in the cab of the diesel-hauled 'Condor' container train. At Carlisle he spent the night in the Train Crew Hostel before returning home the following morning.

About a month later Hugh received a letter stating that the writer had reason to believe he was the H.M. Jenkins who had spent a night in the hostel at Carlisle in the previous month. For a moment there were visions of being disciplined for misusing a footplate pass but relief came when the letter went on to say that only 3s 6d had been charged for his bed and breakfast whereas, as a management trainee, he should have paid the inspectors' rate of 7s. Would he kindly forward the difference!

Sitting Ducks

Carrying huge amounts of extra traffic was not the only contribution made by railways to the war effort in the Second World War. On several occasions they also provided locomotives to be used as targets for aircraft in practice attacks. One location selected for this purpose was the North Pembrokeshire line which had started a long drawn out redundancy when the GWR route to Fishguard opened in 1906. Local passenger services had ended in 1937 and there was no great problem in halting the surviving freight working in June 1944 to allow the US Eighth Air Force to test different types of ammunition on GWR locomotive No.2656. In return for punching thirty-five holes in the whitewashed boiler of the locomotive the US Transportation Corps undertook a miracle repair in its workshops and got 2656 back in service in four days.

In the previous year LNER D21 Class 4-4-0 No.1241 had been painted white at Swindon and then moved to North Pembrokeshire for a similar trainbusting exercise. The tunnel between Rosebush and Maenclochog also featured in the 1943 activity when it was used as a target in bouncing bomb exercises. De Havilland Mosquitos of No.618 Squadron of the RAF made ten low-level attacks at 200mph and two at 300mph and scored nine hits. Two of the 'Highball' bombs whizzed straight through the tunnel!

Dick Hardy

After his motive power years, R.H.N. Hardy became divisional manager at King's Cross. He was not only a first class railwayman but possessed great charisma and a fine sense of humour.

Heading from King's Cross to Peterborough one day for a meeting with the British Sugar Corporation I spotted Dick getting onto the footplate of our locomotive and knew he would be taking a turn at both shovel and regulator during the journey. On the next day we travelled together to a meeting at Hatfield and I could not resist telling Geoff Wilson, who was with us, about a hair-raising journey I'd had the previous day and how some over-enthusiastic engine handling had turned passengers pale, brought luggage down from the racks and flung old ladies from their seats. Dick's face was a picture until I could keep up the pretence no longer and confessed my deception.

In the Dead of Night

In 1984 an InterCity HST power car was named *Darlington* by Councillor Jim Skinner, the local town mayor, at Darlington Bank Top station. Fifty years earlier a rather more unusual christening had taken place at North Road Works there.

The later LNER B17 4-6-0 locomotives were being given the names of first and second division football teams but, languishing in a lower division, the local club would not share in this process. However, a few stalwart supporters among the local railway staff decided to take matters into their own hands. The works' night shift stripped the nameplates off *Manchester City* and sent the locomotive out next morning carrying their home-produced *Darlington* plates instead!

There was a happy ending for so good was the workmanship involved in this illicit 'ringing' that the LNER management agreed to name another B17 *Darlington* if the *Manchester City* plates were put back.

LNER 4-6-0 locomotive No.2830 *Thoresby Park* photographed from the long through platform at Cambridge station.

Cambridge

Cambridge was a great place for motive power variety and a favourite haunt for trainspotters. It was unusual anyway in having a long, single main platform with a central crossover for access and double bays at each end for local services. The north end bays served Kettering, St Ives, Mildenhall and Ipswich trains while the two at the south end handled the services to King's Cross and on the ex-LNW route to Bletchley. Along with the B17s, graceful Claud 4-4-0s and their impressive Holden 4-6-0 big brothers worked the most important trains on the ex-GE section routes with E4 2-4-0s mostly handling the lightly loaded workings to Marks Tey and Mildenhall. During my time at Cambridge I had a room in a garret belonging to a delightful old couple who insisted on supplementing my rent payments by beating me at rummy most evenings!

FIFTEEN

COMEDY AND CHARACTERS

Any organisation is only as good as its people and railways employed a large number of exemplary people. Quite a few of them were outstanding professionally and others just outstanding as people. Despite an ingrained dedication to providing safe transport railwaymen still found scope for ingenuity and humour in their working environment.

The Yardmasters

I worked with two yardmasters, both great railwaymen and great characters. Harry Onyon was a bluff Lincolnshire man who succeeded in the tough job of running Whitemoor mechanised marshalling yard by sheer knowledge, common sense and fairness. He eventually achieved that career pinnacle, appointment as the stationmaster at Liverpool Street and was as good at welcoming royalty or dealing with disputes among the parcels staff as he had been with keeping the wagons moving through his bleak Fenland yard. His system? Tiny, abbreviated reminders written on a single sheet of paper and not crossed off until fully dealt with.

Harry's first London appointment was as yardmaster at Temple Mills where he took over from Dan Rose who had just successfully steered the yard from a traditional flat shunting conglomeration into a modern new hump yard. Dan was just so experienced that he was able to run the shunting activity at Temple Mills as if it were his own empire, successfully flouting any attempts at HQ interference by blinding people with his incredible memory and knowledge. In contrast to Harry's measured calm Dan was all movement, words and fire. Cunning came into the equation, too, for he would ask the West Yard Hump cabin whether the shunting signal for the main hump was off and, if not, ring the hump inspector and fire off the words, 'Why aren't you shunting; get on with it'.

When he took over the new, modern Temple Mills marshalling yard complex Harry found that the Guards' Dormitory was not really needed in light of the improved freight train pattern. He did offer me, as one of his assistant yard masters at the time, the opportunity to buy at a knocked-down price the forty-nine redundant GER-crested chamber pots but, fearing to take these home to my respectable suburban semi, I declined. I do sometimes wonder if I was right in view of the prices antiques now command.

Bucket Trouble

Each morning in the West of England Divisional Office, the divisional manager would review the activities of the previous twenty-four hours. On one such occasion Henry Sanderson was palpably annoyed by an incident in which a bucket of ballast had been left on the Down main line during the night. Reading from the Control Log he listed the damage caused to a train by this oversight, 'couplings buckled, heating pipes ripped off and damage to coach batteries…'

Dan Reynolds, the traction officer and known for his unassuming manner and quiet humour, was heard to mutter to another member of the management team, 'I don't suppose it did the bucket any good either!'

Succinct Reporting

An apocryphal story from Tasmanian Railways concerned a stationmaster called Lonnagin. On appointment to a station with a reputation for derailments, he was advised to keep reports on any such incident brief and to the point as his immediate superior hated wordiness. Taking the advice to heart, the new appointee is said to have reported his first derailment by telegraph in the following terms: 'Off agin, on agin, gone agin, Lonnagin.'

Only on the Great Western

The old Great Western was a paternalistic enterprise, noted for its characters right from the days of Brunel and Gooch. Many of its senior officers were noted, and generally admired, for their idiosyncracies and were treated with great respect by the staff.

After the GWR150 celebrations of the Great Western's 150th anniversary in 1985 former Prime Minister Harold Macmillan was the speaker at a dinner to mark the successful conclusion of the various events that had been staged to mark the occasion. With his own special magic the speaker reminisced about his time as a director of the Great Western Railway and painted a hilarious picture of the procession of wheelchairs, canes and companions needed to get all the aged members of the board into a meeting.

On one occasion Mr Macmillan had travelled by train to Cornwall for a meeting. Not in the best of health at the time he had been touched by the provision of a wheelchair to carry him from the train to a waiting car and asked, 'Do you treat all Prime Ministers this way?' 'Oh no sir,' came the porter's reply, 'only Great Western directors.'

There was undoubtedly what would now be considered abuse of privilege but the general managers of the GWR ran their railway like the textile barons of the north and took the privileges as being no more than their due for running a successful business. One general manager went to most of the race meetings on his system, using his own saloon and frequently borrowing £10 from his subordinates for the day's betting.

Talking about his appointment later on as general manager of the Western Region, Freddie Wright recalled telling his father, an ex-North Eastern man, the news. 'But that's a gentleman's job,' was the response.

It was commonly supposed that Stanley Raymond's appointment to the WR post was specifically to change its feudal culture. For those who continued to act as if the old days still existed a new breed of manager throughout the Divisions had a way of cutting them down to size. In one such case a senior visitor from Paddington who insisted on being entertained in a strip club asked for directions to the loo. The directions given led him straight into the girls' dressing rooms and a chorus of protest that must have been heard as far away as Penzance.

The Old Stories are the Best

Many a meandering local railway has been the scene for the heavily pregnant passenger who anxiously enquires of the guard, 'How much longer will we be? Can't you see I'm pregnant?' He is concerned but can't resist saying, 'You were really not very wise to take a train like this in your condition.' With resignation she responds, 'I know, but I wasn't in this condition when I got on!'

Dambuster

At one time members of a friend's family lived in the crossing house at Single Hill, between Bath and Radstock on the old Somerset & Dorset Joint line. As in most such homes a good fire in the hearth depended upon generous enginemen supplementing the official allowance by helping coal to fall from the tender of a passing locomotive from time to time. Single Hill was on a curve and it only needed a clever prod with the shovel to shoot a sizeable lump off in such a way that it would land conveniently near the coal bunker at the back of the crossing house.

One day it all went wrong, however, and the clever prod was a little too energetic. Like the Dambuster's bouncing bomb the coal sailed outwards in a magnificent curve, skidded on the wet cottage lawn and burst through the door of the outdoor lavatory to the great alarm of the astonished, but fortunately uninjured, occupant.

Mistaken Identity

A passenger who joined the overnight sleeper at Euston on one occasion was very drunk and insisted on instructing the sleeping car attendants to wake him before Carlisle, help him dress and make sure he alighted there. A generous tip helped to keep the matter in the forefront of their minds.

On arrival at Glasgow the two attendants were discussing the journey when they were horrified to see the same passenger approaching them. He was furious and threatened to report them both. Eventually he stormed off leaving one attendant to observe wryly to the other, 'He can't be half as mad as the chap we persuaded to dress and leave the train at Carlisle!'

Negotiations in Cornwall

Selling railway transport in Cornwall was quite different to such activities elsewhere, partly because of the spirit of independence reigning in Kernow and partly because its geographic isolation inflicted higher rates and fares on the county. The former showed through when Peter Nicholls was taken by local salesman Donald James to visit the Old Delabole Slate Co. to see if there was any more freight traffic to be had from them. The BR men were shown round the works and then adjourned to the office for their discussions. As it happened to be the day that Prime Minister Ted Heath had signed up for Europe, Peter asked whether the change would encourage Old Delabole to seek wider markets. 'Well,' came the reply, 'we already deal with the Frenchies and the Germans, it's only they bloody Devonians I can't stand.'

Being invited to a meal with the chairman of Cornwall County Council was like an engagement with royalty – menus with each guest's name and all the other trimmings. However, the annual meeting with the broccoli growers to discuss rates for the substantial seasonal rail movements could be very different. Like the one with the daffodil growers it could get quite lively. Among the other challenges was a project to move great mounds of waste china clay sand in huge trainloads for use as building blocks.

Another major traffic flow was that of early flowers grown in the Isles of Scilly and put on rail at Penzance. This, too, involved annual negotiations over rates and a visit to St Mary's for discussions with the Isles of Scilly Steamship Co. in their capacity as agents for bringing the traffic over. The company's senior people were always charming, helpful and hospitable, but were also tough negotiators. Trevor Anderson and Peter Nicholls only got the increase of a halfpenny a box they needed in one session by using Peter to match the imbibing of the Steamship Co. representative while Trevor presented the arguments. They got their increase at 3 a.m. when Trevor inconveniently remembered that their next meeting was in Truro in just a few hours time.

An earlier such session involved the author who was also provided with a superb meal in the company's offices followed by amicable but tough negotiations on into the evening. What my hosts failed to mention was that, at that time, all the street lights went out at 10 p.m. and an hilarious search for a misplaced hotel in a strange town in complete darkness made my visit particularly memorable.

Unchained Provost

Lord Aberdeen used to tell a story set in Kintore. Although a junction on the Great North of Scotland's main line, north of Aberdeen the station was rarely very busy. It was, however, a Royal Burgh and very proud of that fact. This was explained to an impatient traveller who asked a porter standing just outside his compartment why the train bothered to stop at such a quiet place. He was told that not only was Kintore a Royal Burgh but that it had its own Provost. The passenger asked whether he went about with a chain. 'Na, he jist gangs aboot loose,' he was assured.

The Stationmasters

One stationmaster on the GN&GE Joint line between March and Sleaford had an unenviable reputation for meanness and for abusing his position. The Christmas gifts and gratuities that came to most stations in those days were not shared with the staff; porters were bullied into digging the garden of the station house and the chickens he kept were fed entirely on loose grain from the goods shed, even if it meant holing a few sacks for the purpose.

Eventually the station staff rebelled against this oppressive regime. Nothing overt or punishable, of course; that was not the way it was done. Instead, a trail of corn was laid from the goods shed to the main line, a few luckless chickens reached the table prematurely and a petty official learned a small lesson.

The stationmaster's pride and joy was his peaked cap with the magic words 'Station Master' embroidered in gold. One bald stationmaster in the Plymouth district was said never to remove his while another Plymouth man, the portly stationmaster at Friary, even added a white top, naval fashion, during the summer months. The career pinnacle for stationmasters was appointment to one of the high-status stations where the uniform issued included a silk hat and morning dress for such special occasions as welcoming royalty and VIPs. In BR days there were twenty-six posts in this category, ten of them in London.

Common sense and initiative were essential qualities for a good stationmaster. They were exemplified at Pitsea in the 1960s when a local bus operator began leaving one of his vehicles in the station car park without either permission or payment. Requests to stop the practice or pay for it producing no result, the stationmaster made his point by turning out late one night and chaining the bus to a lamp post.

A good stationmaster only invoked the formal disciplinary procedure if absolutely necessary. On one occasion a porter in the Worcester area was

In addition to the huge commuter business the station master at Liverpool Street was responsible for looking after royalty travelling to and from Sandringham and for foreign dignitaries arriving on the boat trains from Parkeston Quay.

rostered to clip three sets of catch points at Honeybourne to permit an engineer's possession of the line. The job was important, especially as a slip up the previous week had resulted in a derailment. Unfortunately the porter allocated to do the work reported for duty late and rather drunk. Instead of issuing a formal reprimand the stationmaster took the unhappy porter part way by car and then made him tramp across muddy fields, along boggy tracks and through windswept and rain-lashed cuttings until he finally reached the points he had to clamp in a bedraggled but sober and wiser condition.

Well Named

Jim Burnham tells of an incident from his days as a summer relief clerk back in 1947, a time when there were still many USAAF air bases operational in East Anglia. On a glorious Monday morning in August, the staff at Haughley station were awaiting the arrival of their new stationmaster, Joseph Pilgrim. He was known as a strict disciplinarian and a highly pious man and Reg Smith, who had been relieving in the post, had warned everyone to create a good impression.

Around midday the new man was taken on a tour of his 'empire', Down side first, then the goods yard and the signal box at the junction with the Mid-Suffolk Light Railway, and finally back along the Up platform to the booking office. Passing the waiting room Reg had tried to divert his replacement from seeing a young lady 'close coupled' with an American airman but had not succeeded. Back in the office Mr Pilgrim demanded an explanation of this scene of female wickedness. Cheerfully Reg explained, 'Ah yes, that would be your late turn booking clerk, Miss Bedworthy!'

Moving Trains

I stopped jumping on or off moving trains after witnessing a passenger getting off one of the old steam-era suburban sets working into Moorgate and falling between the platform and the carriage running board. I can still hear his agonised 'Oh my God!'

On a lighter note is that time-honoured tale of the passenger racing along the platform at King's Cross, scrambling into the last carriage of the departing train and shouting to a porter, 'OK for Finsbury Park?' 'Yes,' came the reply. 'Change at Peterborough!'

Punctuality

According to the late Charles Clinker the old GWR was very good at train running but surprisingly poor at station working. Former WR Operations Manager Bob Poynter found that little had changed when he took charge of Kemble station for a while after finishing his Traffic Apprentice training. At the time Kemble was a busy junction where the railbus-worked branch lines from Cirencester and Tetbury met the main line from Gloucester to Swindon. The station was a calling point for the Cheltenham Spa Express which was booked to depart at 9.04 a.m. Finding that, as he put it, 'the station working was very leisurely' Bob took to blowing his whistle just before departure time to ensure that this important train got away promptly.

For a day or two the new system worked without a hitch, but then a car announced its impending arrival with a fanfare of horn blowing followed by a screeching halt outside the station entrance, just as the tail lamp of the express vanished in the direction of Swindon. An elegant blonde lady stormed into the station demanding to know why the stationmaster had allowed it to leave without her. Unimpressed by Bob's explanation of the need for punctuality she told him that she had an arrangement that when she blew the horn of her car the station staff would hold the train for her!

"MORE HASTE LESS SPEED"   Copyright.

Bob, who had a lively sense of humour, could not keep a straight face after hearing this but he did manage to restore good customer relations with a cup of coffee and a couple of telephone calls.

Whistle-blowing failed to cure a similar problem when Bob moved to Twyford, especially with the through trains off the Henley branch. Closing the ticket barrier just before departure time was tried instead and worked well until the day that the early turn ticket collector forgot and had to use his outstretched arm to prevent a late arrival jumping on to a moving train. Smartly, the would-be traveller ducked beneath it but not low enough to prevent his bowler hat from coming off and rolling down the platform. Faced with a choice between catching the train or his favourite headgear the latter won – by a head!

Dai's Ambition

Dai had been a signalman for a long time but had recently begun to feel the stirrings of ambition. He decided to apply for promotion and in due course was called for interview by the district officer.

'Dai,' said the D.O., 'I want you to imagine that you are in charge of a signal box on a single line of railway. One day you find out that a train is heading towards you from each direction. What would you do?'

'I'd put all my signals to danger,' responded Dai promptly.

'But suppose they were all faulty,' argued the interviewing officer.

'Why, in that case I'd run up the line and place detonators in each direction,' came Dai's confident response.

'Yes, but the detonators have got damp and won't work,' was the next obstacle.

'Then I'd wave a red flag from the window of my signal box,' came back Dai, with a note of triumph in his voice.

But his tormentor had not finished. 'But your flags have been chewed up by rats,' he persisted. For a moment Dai looked defeated as he pondered the predicament but then brightened up and produced his ace rejoinder.

'In that case, I'd dash over to our cottage,' said Dai, 'and shout from the bottom of the stairs, "Blodwen, if you want to see the biggest bloody smash up you've ever seen get down here quickly!"'

Each Way Bet

Miles away from Dai a local crossing keeper was asked why one of his two crossing gates was across the road and the other across the track. Sagely he explained that he was half expecting a train.

Royal Trains

Guards on the royal trains were always as immaculately turned out as their engines. In more egalitarian times one Southern Region guard who was chosen for the duty but then reproved when he reported for work for in highly informal dress responded, 'Well, I have bought a new pair of daps.'

In recalling the many times he was involved with royal journeys Trevor Anderson talked of happy memories of these occasions and 'especially of the grace and charm of the ladies and the humour of the gentlemen of the household' of Her Majesty. On one occasion when the train failed to stop at the appointed spot at a small country station the welcoming group had to quickly move from the position Trevor had marked with a 'P' to the actual alighting point. When presented to the Prince of Wales Trevor had been asked about the marking and explained that the 'P' stood for Prince. Laughing, HRH commented, 'It would seem to me more appropriate if the "P" had stood for perhaps.'

Collapse of Stout Party

The district engineer at York was using his saloon to take a party on an inspection of the line to Scarborough when it was brought to a halt because a road vehicle had run through some crossing gates. The senior officers descended to offer their portentous advice, among them the signal engineer who was a little inclined to pomposity. 'It only needs a bit of welding,' he told the ganger. Harassed enough already, the latter replied, 'I've a brother in the village who can weld almost anything, starting with your mouth, but these gates are cast iron!'

A Little Bit of Texas

Sir Stanley Raymond presented a highly sceptical view of almost everything and was critical from the moment he arrived to inspect the new Tinsley marshalling yard. At the time it was the latest thing in mechanised yards with variable pressure hydraulic retarders which could both slow down and speed up wagons passing through them. In effect a skilled operator could squeeze a vehicle along.

Among the teething troubles were leaks from the hydraulic system. One occurred just as Sir Stanley was passing; a jet of oil fountained upwards and the alarm went off within the prescribed time. A portly fitter came hurrying up and was asked by the distinguished visitor, 'Does this happen often?' 'Listen mate,' came the frank reply, 'there's more oil around this place than under the whole of Texas.'

Rapid Ageing

The manager of Freightliner's South West area used to visit his depot at Swansea by taking the train to High Street station where depot manager Stan Judd would meet him in the depot's venerable Austin 1300 saloon. There was always much to discuss and the return to High Street was always a last-minute affair. On one well-remembered occasion the mad rush through the back doubles led Stan to observe proudly, 'When we left it was 39 [meaning minutes past the hour] and now its 43.' The heartfelt response was, 'When we left I was 39, but now I feel 43!'

Spoken For

In west Wales many people speak in their native Welsh tongue, in which *gwr* means married man. Innocent young girls had been known to appreciate the fact that uniformed GWR staff clearly displayed their marital status on their caps.

Overcarried

A Fleet Street newsman regularly travelled home on a late train from St Pancras to Harpenden. One night he was just so tired that he overslept and did not wake until the train reached Bedford. Catching the next train south he again overslept and failed to wake before it got to St Pancras.

Annoyed and embarrassed by this incident he determined that there should be no repetition and, on the next homeward journey, pinned a notice on his coat asking that if he slept he should be woken at Harpenden. Instead he again woke at Bedford, to find that someone had added 'Ha, ha!' to his notice.

Retaliation

Railwaymen have never tolerated idlers and scroungers for long. One guard who regularly worked an Up market goods train and was relieved en route made a habit of filling his can from any unattended brew. When this was one day made with senna pods the uncomfortable journey home cured him of the bad practice.

Time for Tea

From a train waiting for a connection late at night a man asked a porter on the Norfolk station, 'Do I have time for a cup of tea,' and got a prompt reply, 'Yes, thet yew hev.' After searching vainly for the refreshment room he found the porter again and said, 'I thought you said I could get a cup of tea.' Patiently the railwayman responded, 'No, bor. Oi said yew'd got time fer one. I never sed yew could git one.'

Dire Consequences

Bananas disappeared from the British table during the war but at the end of hostilities Bristol was among the first places to see them once again. The first supplies arrived onboard the SS *Tilapa* in December 1945 and were met at Avonmouth Docks by the Lord Mayor of the city and a huge welcoming crowd. For some time a Banana Order restricted consumption to one a week for children and expectant mothers but the trade eventually resumed its old level. Millions of bananas on 'hands' and 'stems' were then imported through Avonmouth and unloaded there to wagons or for local distribution. Dry ice was used to prevent premature ripening on the way to ripening sheds throughout the country and it was good traffic for railways, apart from the odd poisonous spider or beetle found among the cargoes.

A little boy travelling by train on the Avonmouth branch at the time banana imports were resumed was given his first banana just before the train passed into the tunnel under Clifton Downs. As he took his first bite the carriage was plunged into semi-darkness disturbed only by his howl of dismay and complaint that the banana had made him go blind.

The Monday Club

Bob Hilton was a strong, forceful character and during his time as divisional manager at Cardiff his senior staff formed an informal group known as 'The Monday Club'. Membership consisted of those Bob had bawled out for some shortcoming or other at his regular Monday review meetings.

SIXTEEN

WORD POWER

Due to its size and complexity the railway system was extremely word and communication dependent. There is no way of calculating the words appearing in the various instructional books alone but just one subject on one railway, the operational data in the LNER's General Appendix, for example, required 468 foolscap pages to record. The areas of performance, finance and other recording, the posters, handbills and other publicity material and the day to day process of direction and control all added to this word dependence. Staff records, paybills, equipment maintenance and a hundred other areas of activity kept printers busy, filing cabinets full and the stores people issuing thousands of forms, pens, pencils and so on.

The way in which ordinary words are used can sometimes put a whole different slant on an otherwise ordinary situation and with so many words floating about the railway systems cases of this sort were inevitable.

Bad News and Good News

An InterCity 125 HST set had failed completely on the East Coast Main Line in the period before its electrification. In line with the best customer relations practice the senior conductor used his communication system to advise passengers of the situation. With imagination, inspiration and humour he announced that he had both bad news and goods news for them:

> The bad news is that both engines of the train have failed; the good news is that this is not a Boeing 757.

Esprit de Corps

For many years the railways had their own docks at Poplar in East London, with the North London, Great Northern, Great Western, Midland and LNW companies all having depots there. The area was terribly mauled during the Blitz but was busy again in BR days, the London Midland Region dealing with traffic to and from ships and lighters at Poplar Dock (North) and the Eastern Region at Poplar Dock (South).

As part of one of the many rationalisations of the 1960s and 1970s the whole dock area was transferred to Eastern Region control and the ER goods agent became responsible for all operations. Not long after the changes a temporary traffic situation meant that he had to ask one of the ex-LMR dock crane drivers to leave his normal post of operating a 3-ton crane and work briefly on one of the higher capacity 5-ton ones. The employee agreed but asked whether there would be any financial recognition of the change expecting, perhaps, some modest overtime. His boss saw the matter as just a normal need for flexibility and, to avoid the issue getting contentious, replied jocularly that he could book a couple of hours 'esprit de corps'. Unsure of what was meant, the crane driver replied, 'But we never had that on the London Midland, Guv'nor.'

This story was widely relished in Eastern Region circles!

A dockside crane unloads starch from the SS *Snottering* at East Quay, Poplar Dock, on 16 July 1963.

The Train Indicator

Stations which served holiday camps at places like Minehead, Pwllheli, Skegness and Clacton used to be incredibly busy on summer Saturdays. Many extra trains arrived and departed and one of the preparation tasks was to draw up a schedule of what each arriving engine, stock and guard was supposed to work next. Of course, if the first inwards train arrived late, the plan collapsed in domino fashion and the stationmaster and his supervisors were forced to improvise, tell Control what they had done and hope everything worked out for the best.

Departing passengers used to form long queues outside the station at Clacton-on-Sea where the concourse platform indicator was crucial to directing people to the right train. Of the old-fashioned type with destinations printed on wooden boards that slotted into place as required, the station got its supplies of new or replacement boards from Stratford Stores if their request was approved by Liverpool Street. One request that failed to get such approval was an order for 'Spare sluts for the use of station staff.'

The Welcome Wagon

The Welcome Wagon was a scheme in which local women were employed on a part-time basis to call upon new arrivals to an area and welcome them with a collection of small gifts provided by commercial sponsors. They might dispense bus timetables, small proprietary items, a street map and other useful things that would also reflect commercial credit on the providers. In each area a supervisor negotiated the inclusion of sponsors into the scheme, recruited the female gift distributors and planned their workload.

BR's West of England Division joined the scheme a little before the arrival of its new sales manager who bought a house in the area and started using it before his family moved down from Worcester. It seemed entirely appropriate that the Welcome Wagon should call and surprise him but, to make the occasion memorable, the normal gifts were replaced by a huge basket with unusual contents. With great goodwill the beautiful, dancer daughter of the Welcome Wagon supervisor agreed to pose in it holding a bottle of champagne.

Responding to the doorbell the new member of the division's management team showed a moment of stark astonishment but recovered very quickly with the phrase, 'Can I keep her?' No, he could not; but he did get the normal welcome pack.

His colleagues thought it best not to tell his wife!

The Welcome Wagon
calls on Bristol's new
sales manager, the late
Trevor Anderson.

Book Theft

The Public Relations team at Eastern Region headquarters at York had a
reputation for imagination, enterprise and humour. This got turned on their
general manager because he never got round to returning books borrowed
from the PR office. They waited until he had gone out and then made good
use of a newly made rubber stamp embossed 'This book was stolen from the
Public Relations office, York.'

Graffiti

Graffiti is deplorable and costs railway organisations vast sums of money
to remedy, but occasionally it offers a novel thought that is a slight
compensation for the damage caused. One is bound to be just a little
touched by the plaintive message left by a woebegone trainspotter at a
station on the main line just north of King's Cross. This read simply, 'Died
waiting for Cicero'. Presumably he had 'clocked' most of the A3 Pacifics
and marked them off in the current Ian Allan numbers book but had not
managed to catch No.600101 *Cicero*.

A soldier, less than enchanted with army life, was probably responsible for one of the most unkind graffito examples. In a coach on one of the Reading–Tonbridge sets the official notice asking passengers not to use the toilet when the train was standing in a station carried an addition which read 'Except at Aldershot'.

At one time there was an on-going reaction to the London Transport warning 'Bill Stickers Will Be Prosecuted'. It began with 'Bill Stickers is Innocent' and culminated with the demand 'Free Bill Stickers'.

One of the most touching examples of these unofficial messages appeared at various locations in the south west and read simply: 'Brunel Rules, OK'.

Steamy Statistics

A story circulating in a railway consultancy firm concerned a North American company considering a move into transportation in the 'new' Russia. They narrowed their interest down to a railway undertaking and, after some preliminary discussions, faxed their target with a long list of detailed questions designed to help in moving the matter forward. One called for details of the railway's staff, broken down by sex but, somehow, the question was misconstrued. After a lengthy interval the return fax stated that 'sex was not the problem, it was alcohol!'

Firing Line

In Britain experiments with rail-mounted guns date back to an 1894 trial on the LB&SC at Newhaven, with the union between railways and artillery the subject of further liaison in both world wars. Despite problems of weight and recoil a number of heavy guns were mounted on railway wagons and operated by Royal Artillery teams in conjunction with professional railwaymen. As so often happens with such highly individual units many of the guns were given official or unofficial names, including *Boche-Buster* for a huge ex-naval gun, *Scene-Shifter* for its partner, and *Piece-Maker* and *Gladiator* for another pair. Records of blast damage to track and local housing plus at least one case of recoil setting the gun wagon in motion suggest that putting heavy guns on railway wagons was not without its difficulties!

Paybills

Railway pay has always been complicated due to the variety of jobs, grades and other factors affecting railway staff. By 1990, for example, the payslip codes allocated to the various pay allowances and deductions had risen to no less than 988. No.988 itself referred to 'Attachment of Earnings Orders'.

Allowances had proliferated with the arrival of the bonus years and the increasing recognition that a public service entailed working unsocial hours or in unsocial conditions. Allowances for night and Sunday duty, or for being 'On Call' featured in the list alongside 'Nurse's Laundry Allowance' and 'Signalmen's Isolation Payment'. Among the especially intriguing examples were the 'Skills Retention Payment' and the 'Minder Allowance Payment'.

The range of deductions was just as varied. The L&Y Sick Fund Society and the Doncaster LNER Motor Ambulance Fund received members' contributions via the paybills which also coped with loans, garden rents and officers' mess bills. Among the unusual items were those involving the Southern Goodwill Society and the scheme for Apprentices' Tool Repayments.

Fortunately modern technology was well able to handle all these complexities. A total of 150,000 payslips – some 6 miles of paper weighing over 8cwt – could be laser printed in less than five hours.

Delicately Put

Doubtful punctuation and curious précis were a standard feature of control logs but the occasional example of delicacy also appeared. In one case, where a train had stopped to allow the guard to receive medical attention, the log recorded that the unfortunate man 'slipped and his hind quarters went through a window' resulting in deep cuts to 'his upper leg'.

Le Cerf

The British Eurostar driver had seen a deer on the line on the French portion of his journey and needed to convey the information to the French signaller. Unfortunately he just could not recall the French for deer but got round the problem by advising the astonished *cheminot* that there was 'a horse on the line with its pantograph up'!

Gloomy Prediction

Just before his retirement a long-serving signalman, noted for his pessimistic outlook, was visited by the district inspector who congratulated him on his thirty-eight years of service in the same box. 'I'll be longer in the next one,' came the gloomy reply.

The Weekly Returns

Every station and depot had to submit a pink form explaining variations in passenger revenue and a yellow one for freight. In the district office these were used as a basis for more reporting up the chain. Some stations never managed to identify the reasons for an increase or decrease in business while others resorted to such unhelpful generalisations as 'more passengers this year'.

This was not so in Edington Burtle, a lonely place on the Somerset Levels which had been Edington Junction until the branch line to Bridgwater was closed. After that users were few and far between so that it was easy to explain why, in one return, the receipts were £6 higher than in the same week a year earlier. 'Passenger to Waterloo this year' in the explanation column of the form said it all.

Tops and Bottoms

In 1956 the days of the Plymouth Train Office were coming to an end. A great deal of change was in the air, including TOPS (Total Operations Processing Scheme) which was on the horizon. This would provide complete control over freight traffic movement and dramatically cut the number of people previously engaged in monitoring wagon movements and searching for missing ones. A TOPS pilot scheme was about to be introduced at Exeter and was the topic of the day in the trains office where staff knew their days were numbered but remained cheerful about the future. However, the man in charge did say that he felt TOPS was not the way forward; what about BOTTOMS – 'Back off to the old manual system'.

SEVENTEEN

THE RAILWAY LANGUAGE

As happened in many large industries railwaymen developed their own special language. A mixture of familiarity, whimsy and practicality, it had many years in which to attain the colourful, fairly universal in-status it had achieved before the advent of rapidly increasing technology and operational streamlining reversed the vogue.

To an outsider or newcomer this private language undoubtedly seemed both curious and exclusive but it was a fact of life. To hear a signalman say 'I've dyked the pick-up and arranged for the cripple to be knocked off The Biscuits so we can let the Parly go' and know what was meant gave a warm sense of belonging. To say 'The pick-up goods train has been shunted into a siding and we are detaching a defective wagon from the train conveying Huntley & Palmer's biscuits so that the all-stations passenger train can proceed' seems a bit wordy and stuffy by comparison.

The Individual Railways

Several individual railway companies had generally affectionate names that reflected their territory. Calling the Great Eastern Railway the 'Swedie', for example, was a clear reference to the swede crops of its agricultural homeland. 'Lanky' was used to denote the Lancashire & Yorkshire company, 'Wessie' the London & North Western and 'Derby' the Midland Railway because its headquarters were there. The North Staffordshire was 'The Knotty', a reference to the Staffordshire Knot, and for some curious reason the Great Central was 'The Pug' and the Midland & South Western Junction enterprise 'The Tiddly (or Diddly) Dyke'.

Derogatory names abounded like 'Old Worse & Worse' for the Oxford, Worcester & Wolverhampton company, 'Muddle & Go Nowhere' for the M&GN and 'Money Sunk & Lost' for the Manchester, Sheffield & Lincolnshire enterprise. Rather gentler was the 'Slow, Easy & Comfortable' soubriquet for the South Eastern & Chatham system. The LNER was either the 'Late & Never Early' or the 'London & Nearly Everywhere' railway, the latter possibly a reference to that fact that its maps gave this impression by showing lines over which the company had running powers as well as those it owned. The Somerset & Dorset Railway was either 'Slow & Dirty' or 'Swift & Delightful' depending on your perspective or journey experience.

There were three alternatives in the case of the Great Western Railway, 'God's Wonderful Railway', 'Great Way Round' – a reference to the original route via Bristol – and 'Go When Ready', possibly a sarcastic comment on the somewhat leisurely practices at some rural locations. Author George Behrend added 'Gone With Regret', and created as fine a book title as anyone could wish for.

Locomotives

A system with American origins that used a locomotive's wheel arrangement to give a generic name to all designs of the same wheel profile was widely used in Britain. Thus, all locomotives with four leading wheels, six coupled driving wheels and two wheels trailing beneath the cab, i.e. 4-6-2s, were 'Pacifics', 2-6-0s 'Moguls' and 4-4-2s 'Atlantics'. However, going far beyond this was the railwayman's habit of giving more graphic names to almost anything, a practice applied with considerable imagination to the various classes of locomotive.

The striking Raven 4-6-2s of the North Eastern Railway were certainly 'Pacifics' but working staff referred to them as 'Skittle Alleys' because of their length, while the Franco-Crosti boiler version of the huge BR standard Class 9 2-10-0s were generally known as 'Combine Harvesters', again a reference to size. Outward appearance also resulted in locomotive types being labelled 'Fat Nannies', 'Humpty Dumpties', 'Spam Cans' or 'Hikers'. The 0-8-4T engines hauling coal trains from Wath yard bore no resemblance to flowers but were universally known as 'Wath Daisies'.

Running characteristics provided the inspiration for another group of names producing examples such as 'Gobblers' for the coal-hungry GER M15 2-4-2 tanks and 'Buckjumpers' for the 0-6-0s which were pretty lively when starting with the regulator fully open. The vogues of the times produced the names 'Tangos', 'Ragtimers' and 'Jazzers', while electric locomotives as a group became 'Sparkers' and diesel locomotives 'Growlers'. The GWR Brown Boveri gas turbine locomotive No. 18000 was often called the 'Kerosene Castle'.

The Great Northern's N2 tank engines were known as 'Breadwinners' because of the volume of work they got through on suburban trains. Less flatteringly the Sentinel steam railcars were frequently referred to as 'Fish and Chip Vans', and one LNWR class of freight locomotives was sometimes known as 'Bill Baileys' because, like the song, they often failed to come home!

Locomotive men added their own expressions to describe working situations, phrases like 'Catch the Water' for priming and 'Blow Up' for the process of creating a brake vacuum. 'Hard up' meant short of steam and 'Dead' was unusable. 'On the Cushions' referred to enginemen travelling by passenger train, always in the compartment nearest to the engine so that they could be contacted if required, while 'hanging on the pot' referred to causing deliberate delay in order to secure overtime or to avoid having to put the engine away as a result of getting back to shed too soon. 'Miners' Friend' was the term for a driver with a reputation for working his engine hard.

Trains

Well might officialdom offer passengers resounding train titles like 'Flying Scotsman' and 'The Hook Continental' or 'Golden Arrow' but this did nothing to stop regular and distinctive trains acquiring their own informal

LNER Atlantic locomotive No.4441 pulls away from Cambridge at the head of a Cambridge Buffet Express, informally known as a 'Beer Train'.

names. Examples include the 1.30 p.m. Paddington to Penzance which was known as 'The Honeymooner' because of the number of newlyweds it carried to the resorts of Devon and Cornwall.

At the other end of the prestige scale was 'The Soap' (or 'Carbolic') which took workers to their employment via Port Sunlight Halt. Further north 'The Paddy' regularly conveyed Irish arrivals from the ferry at Stranraer to London, while 'The Glesga' Paddy' took others in the opposite direction. 'Brain Trains' were those on the cross-country route which linked Oxford and Cambridge and trains on a local service into Glasgow were named after the 'Tinto' hill in Lanarkshire.

There is a nice story behind a return service from Swansea to Penclawd that was called 'The Relish'. Apparently the name was linked to the activities of local women who collected cockles in the Loughor estuary and then took them into the market at Swansea for sale. If they had a good day there would be food treats on the table when they got back, something for the family to 'relish'.

Night journeys between Penzance and Paddington produced the names 'Waker' for the 9 p.m. Up departure and 'Owl' for the Down train which left London at midnight. 'The Zulu' and 'The Limited' were other GWR prime services akin to 'The Corridor' on the LNW.

Local trains were not excluded from this naming process but their appellations tended to be rather less imposing with examples like 'The Marlow Donkey', 'The Tivvy (Tiverton) Bumper' and 'Stratford Jack', the latter a late-1800s shoppers' shuttle service between Victoria Park and Stratford Market. Another shuttle service, the one between Clapham Junction and Kensington, was known as 'The Kenny Flyer', while the one between Audley End and Saffron Walden acquired a somewhat questionable intimacy as 'The Walden Ripper'. 'Monkey Specials' conveyed youngsters to Clifton Down station for a visit to Bristol Zoo and special trains for anglers came to be known as 'Kipper Trips'.

Remembering that railway freight traffic used to earn much more than the passenger business it is fitting that goods trains also received special names. 'The Biscuit' conveyed Huntley & Palmer's forwardings from Reading, 'The Pig' carried pig iron from Bilston and 'The Beer' handled the brewery despatches from Burton-on-Trent.

Highly descriptive was the use of 'The Panic' for the service conveying motor parts from Swindon to Longbridge Works, its name reflecting the urgency of keeping the car production lines fed. High Wycombe was known for the fact that several major furniture manufacturers had their works there and, not too surprisingly, the goods train which carried much of their output was 'The Chairs'. There was even a case of a double naming with the 9.15 p.m. Up working from Bristol which picked up Fry's traffic at Bath being known as 'The Cocoa' and the return 8.43 a.m. from Acton called 'The Ice Cream' because it handled the Walls factory output.

A Whitemoor guard gave his name, 'Freddie Free', to a train he regularly worked, while the Barnwood-Lawley Street 'Snod' got its name from the fact that its regular guard did a bit of shoe repairing on the journey! The 5.8 p.m. from Workington was known as 'The Bond' because a guard of that name worked it for many years.

Places

The two large SR loco sheds in London inevitably got informal diminutives. Thus Stewarts Lane was always known as 'The Lane' and Bricklayers Arms as 'The Brick'. These were not quite as romantic, or as far fetched, as calling Somers Town Goods – a gloomy place if ever there was one - 'The Tea Gardens', but then neither was 'The Lawn' entirely appropriate for the concourse at Paddington.

On the Settle–Carlisle route the line rises to 1,150ft above sea level on the stretch from Settle Junction towards Dent station. Over the 15 miles up to Blea Moor Tunnel the gradient is an almost continuous 1 in 100 making it truly 'The Long Drag', especially with a heavy goods train. Equally descriptive was 'Pneumonia Junction' for the very draughty station at Birkenhead Park.

Some place names had odd historic connections like 'Crimea' for sidings at Didcot and 'Klondyke' for several other such locations. The Down avoiding line at Wood Green was 'The Khyber Pass' presumably because it was channelled through a walled cutting, while the jumble of buildings around King's Cross was unkindly called 'The African Jungle'. Doncaster Works was 'The Plant' and BRB headquarters at 222 Marylebone Road 'The Kremlin'. 'The Drain' not only described the King's Cross–Moorgate line and the Waterloo & City underground link but was also applied to the London & South Western's extension west of Salisbury, in this case because of its unhappy financial consequences.

Local Lines

Local lines got local names so it was near-inevitable that the circuitous Norfolk line from Wroxham to County School should be labelled 'Round the World' and more than one seaside branch called the 'Crab & Winkle'. The Andover–Romsey line was apparently referred to as 'The Sprat & Winkle' by the L&SW chairman at a board meeting and the labelling lived

Terminus of the branch line from Wivenhoe to the widening estuary of the River Colne at Brightlingsea, the 'Crab and Winkle' line as locals knew it.

on. In the same area the Salisbury–Wimborne line was 'The Parson & Prawns' and the original circuitous route of the Southampton & Dorchester Railway 'Castleman's Corkscrew' after promoter A.L. Castleman.

'The Potts Line' went out of use when the Shropshire & Montgomeryshire closed, but 'The Middy' lives on among those who still actively cherish the memory of the old Mid-Suffolk Light Railway that ran out of cash and ended in the middle of a field! For some obscure reason the Stamford–Wansford branch was known as 'The Pig & Whistle', while 'Linger & Die' was an unkindly reference to the line from Itchingfield to Shoreham. The Halwill–Torrington line was 'The Burma Road'.

The earlier railways gave their lines publicity names like 'The Cathedral Route' for the GER access to York via Ely and Lincoln. Naming lines as a way of promoting their use then came back into fashion in BR days to give us 'The Wherry Line', 'The Tarka Line' and countless others. Happily the preserved railways have followed the same path to give us examples like 'The Bluebell Railway' and 'The Poppy Line'.

People

Not surprisingly people also figured prominently in the informal railway language. Staff on light duties, for example, were known as 'Green Card' men, an expression derived from the green label affixed to wagons with some defect and in need of repair. A red label was used if such stock could not be moved so anything unserviceable was said to be 'Red-Carded'.

The special teams scouring the system for economies were 'cuttingly' referred to as 'Razor Gangs', Northampton men as 'Shoemakers' and the bowler-hatted commuters of Haslemere as 'The Flour Graders'. 'Trail Boss' seemed an acceptable epithet for a stationmaster but discovering why Traffic Apprentices were seen as 'thrombosis' was more of a shock. The derivation was a reference to a 'disastrous clot moving around the system and behaving unpredictably'!

Traffic controllers were flatteringly referred to as 'The Brains' and inspectors of all types and persuasions as the 'Black Macs'. A single travelling ticket inspector was a 'Jumper' and a group 'The Flying Squad'.

In Use

The code book used by the railway telegraph offices provided some convenient abbreviations which passed into working conversation; thus 'Caped' was anything cancelled and 'Goosed' anything stopped for a while. The use of 'Foreign' to refer to traffic passing to another railway became legitimised when official paperwork printed a separate column for reporting such traffic. Later 'Hostile Territory' was that of a region other than one's own.

An old railwayman once defined a gentleman as one who tipped half a crown, as opposed to the more normal sixpence or a shilling, and the old railways had a fairly widespread culture of receiving tips. Porters and other staff often performed services well beyond the norm and were, not unreasonably, tipped for doing so, but the practice of actively soliciting tips was frowned upon by most people and was disparagingly referred to as 'Weaselling', 'Fluffing' or, in Scotland, 'Swadging'.

If a passenger 'offered a rabbit to the scuds' it meant he was trying to deceive the ticket inspectors with some sort of alibi ticket. 'Stabling a rake of rough wagons in the refuge' meant putting unsorted traffic into a siding and 'getting a Queen Mary off the kip' was bringing a fitted brake van from the brake siding. 'Things are on the block because they've got one on the floor in the Up Loop but the Bobby has pulled off the board for the Fish and you can cross over when you get the dolly (or dod, dwarf of dummy)' meant that there was traffic congestion due to a derailment in the Up Loop line but the signalman had cleared his signal for the express fish train and the listener could cross the main lines as soon as it had passed and he saw the calling-on signal cleared. Anyone looking for the platelayers at work might well be told to look for them 'in the humpy', their lineside hut.

A 'pick-up' goods train shunting at Lord's Bridge, Cambridgeshire.

But

Stemming from the 1954 Modernisation Plan and the cash it injected into the railway system came a range of increasingly technical equipment. It led to an era of initials like 'dmu' for diesel multiple unit and 'HST' for High Speed Train. Multiple aspect signalling might be functionally referred to as 'mas' but it is hardly as colourful as calling a fixed distant signal 'Forever Amber' after the unchanging colour of its lamp or a toilet seat a 'Launch Pad'.

Despite this change quite a few of the informal railway terms may well be remembered for their sheer novelty. 'The Romford Undertakers' were three Stratford motive power depot foremen who hailed from Romford and dressed in dark suits, railway macs and black homburgs. 'The Rice Pudding Express' was a 1930s noon train from Newcastle to Whitley Bay and 'Perkin's Lighthouse' an oak tree at the top of Etchingham bank on the SE&C route to Hastings, so-called because it represented a haven for enginemen whose engine was running short of steam. Rolling stock in the 1980s Network South East livery of brown and orange got called 'Jaffa Cakes' and the machinery compartments of the Southport electrics owed its graphic description as the 'Death Chamber' to the pyrotechnic display of sparks and flashes as the driver notched up.

EIGHTEEN

ANCILLARY ACTIVITIES

Supplementing and complementing the railways' main commercial, operating and engineering divisions were dozens of other activity groups both within and associated with those spheres or providing their own specialised services.

The two main divisions of engineering activity were the mechanical side, which designed, built, operated and maintained locomotives and rolling stock, and the work of the civil engineers on track and structures. Smaller, but still vital, subdivisions dealt with the signalling and telegraph activity, road motors, outdoor machinery and so on.

The operating officers managed everything to do with train running, from timetable preparation to wagon supply. Their commercial counterparts were responsible for selling the service and charging for goods and passengers and also dealt with such things as publicity, public relations and claims. Both had strong links with the catering, shipping and docks divisions. Staff, accounting and traffic costing officers, too, all had their part to play.

In addition to all these groups there were medical people, legal people, estate and rating surveyors, the British Transport Police, sack and sheet activity staff and many others.

Doing things by Halves

By the beginning of the 1840s the early railways could see a need for an organisation that would divide the receipts from through traffic according to the make up of the route travelled. The outcome was the establishment of the Railway Clearing House in 1842. It grew steadily in line with the expansion of the railway network until its staff numbered nearly 3,000 in the main departments of Merchandise, Coaching and Mileage. It worked through people like the Numbertakers based in marshalling yards and at points of exchange between different railways and used the 'Abstracts' and 'Summaries' forms built into the station clerical reporting process to apportion traffic revenue between the companies.

Over the years the role of the RCH expanded to include issuing publications such as those detailing agreed wagon specifications and the *Handbook of Stations* which listed every station and its facilities. The body also provided a platform for discussing, interpreting and recording commercial and other agreements. These functions continued on into the BR era, although the RCH offices in Eversholt Street never quite lost their slightly stuffy period image.

The traditionalism of the RCH was reflected in its formality and practices. In London, for example, it hosted regular meetings of the various regional commercial managers and provided them with a lunch that included spirits to drink. The managers' group was provided with a bottle of whisky and one of gin but their assistants, who met in advance to prepare for the decision-making of their bosses, were only entitled to half a bottle of each – between half a dozen of them!

Pest Control

Pigeons have long been a thorn in the railway flesh. In the days of grain carriage and storage they found wagons and warehouses to be the pigeon equivalent of five-star living and even in this modern age seem to thrive on fouling newly painted buildings. Nets are one answer to the problem, but Carlisle station has long had a cast-iron figure of an owl atop one of the roof support pillars, probably placed their originally to discourage starlings, another bird nuisance.

At one period the pigeon problem at Poplar Dock got so bad that a major campaign had to be mounted to get rid of them. The line manager's office consulted the boffins at Gidea Park and was advised to use poison bait. Clearly some care was needed in the whole operation but it hardly justified the military-style instructions that were issued and had more in common with a commando raid than with pest clearance. Among the 'begin operations at…' and 'proceed immediately to…' phrases there were detailed arrangements for collecting the carcasses. Not only were staff directed to strategic points around the yard but two men were allocated a dinghy for patrolling the waters of the dock and another got a bicycle for mobile operations in the surrounding streets!

Rabbits, too, can be a problem and one Worcestershire farmer demanded £4,600 in compensation for damage done to his wheat and rape crops by rabbit raids from adjoining BR land. In south Wales the rabbit problem was tackled by licensing wildfowlers to cull the trackside land between Newport and Chepstow. Apparently a ferret named Cuddles proved very effective.

An even greater enemy to foodstuff handling were rodents. One particularly bad infestation of rats was reported in Snow Hill Tunnel at Birmingham. Sure enough the engineer's staff sent out to deal with the problem found rat holes between the sleepers. They chose drowning as the quickest and most effective clearance method, rigged up a hose from the nearest standpipe and poured in water in great quantities. After a suitable interval the water was turned off, the hose rolled up and stored away and the men returned to base for a well-earned cup of tea.

Before the glow of a job well done had begun to fade a freight train emerged from the tunnel and came to a halt beside the South signalbox. The drenched driver and his equally wet mate, in vivid language, reported encountering a burst water main in the tunnel and suggested urgent action. The signalman passed the message on to Control who contacted the stationmaster who, in turn, rang the engineer's staff. The quick-witted response, 'All dealt with, sir,' filled the station master with admiration and earned generous praise for such rapid action.

Tolls

Carriage was not the only business that contributed to the railway coffers. Tolls were levied, and paid out, for all sorts of obscure activities. An example is the toll levied on users of the Haddiscoe New Cut, a man-made waterway linking the rivers Yare and Waveney in the south of Norfolk. It had been completed in 1832 to improve the shipping route from Lowestoft to Norwich, had been acquired by Sir Morton Peto to protect his Lowestoft Railway & Harbour ambitions and eventually passed to the BTC who tried to close it after extensive damage had been caused by the 1953 floods.

Before the new bridge was built over the Cut in 1960 the old bridge had to be raised manually for the passage of trading vessels and pleasure craft and a 2s toll paid for the privilege. A railwayman collected this using a long pole with a net at the end and duly entered the name of the paying vessel in his records so that the money could be taken to account. Being in holiday mood not a few yachtsmen took a delight in the challenge of pitching their coins into the net, not always successfully!

A toll of a different sort was levied at Corby Bridge just east of Carlisle on the line from Newcastle. The old North Eastern Railway allowed pedestrians the use of its viaduct over the River Eden on payment of a halfpenny toll. Magnanimously free passage was granted at church times on Sundays.

On the other side of the balance sheet were tolls like that levied by the Earl of Winchelsea as lord of the manor of Oakham on all coal entering the Oakham lordshold. The original 2d per ton was commuted to £15 a year

'Terrier' No.32661 heads a train over Langstone Bridge on the Hayling Island branch. The road bridge behind was also railway-owned.

when the canal reached Oakham but this toll continued right into BR days and was paid by them as successors to the canal company.

Hayling Island

The 4.5-mile branch line from Havant to Hayling Island opened in 1867. 'The Hayling Billy', as the branch trains were known, had to traverse Langstone Bridge which had a companion road bridge over which the railway was entitled to levy tolls. In the 1940s the Southern Railway's list of tolls featured thirty-eight different charges ranging from a halfpenny for a 'person on foot' (even with a wheelbarrow!) to a half-crown for a hearse with three or more horses and 'with or without a corpse'. Hampshire County Council provided a new road bridge in 1956 but railwaymen continued to collect the tolls there for another four years. The railway itself closed in 1963.

Traffic Courts

The Road & Rail Traffic Act of 1933 made provisions for the railways to lodge an objection in the Traffic Courts to applications made by road hauliers to carry goods for hire or reward. This meant having a small group of staff whose job was to decide which applications ought to be contested to protect railway business and to brief counsel on the grounds for objection and the railway facilities for the traffic in question. In the event of objections being lodged the haulier's application would be heard before the Traffic Commissioner and while the proceedings were normally totally formal they did occasionally produce a moment of humour.

One simple case involved an Essex farmer who wanted a 'B' licence so that he could carry sugar beet to Felstead factory for his neighbours as well as for himself. There were no objections so the Metropolitan Traffic Commissioner asked what radius of operation he wanted included in the conditions of the licence grant. When the farmer seemed uncertain the Commissioner rephrased his enquiry as, 'How far is it to the factory as the crow flies?' The reply, which put a smile on every face in court was, 'I don't know, Your Honour. I've never done it that way!'

Beating the Bounds

The railways' legal and estate and rating departments both had wide-ranging activities. Sometimes these came together as in cases like that of the Ticknall Tramway which was originally built to carry lime for onward conveyance by the Ashby Canal. The Midland Railway acquired the canal in 1846 and to preserve its rights over the tramroad used to work a horse-drawn tram wagon loaded with coal from one end of the branch to the other once every year.

Spike Island

The range of railway fringe activities was enormous, from rubbish disposal at Connington tip to the sheet factory and laundry at Gidea Park. Ticket, stationery and other stores were scattered around the system along with some quite unusual activities like those at Wolverhampton Stafford Road. An isolated area of the works there, known locally as Spike Island, was dedicated to the production of fencing from old locomotive boiler tubes. It got its name from the fact that between the processes of descaling and coating with tar one end of each tube length was cut twice and bent to produce a spike.

Catering

Railway dining could be a memorable experience, especially on a Pullman train or at a railway hotel such as the Tregenna Castle at St Ives. On train staff were especially skilled, like the LMS stewards who used to serve several bowls of soup at once, balancing them on a forearm and making light of a wild descent from Beattock Summit. Station refreshments were rarely of the same standard, especially those offered from platform trolleys where tea plus a rock cake or a piece of slab cake, along with the occasional weary white bread sandwich, was the normal offering.

On the Water

The annual excitement of the author's youthful holidays at Sandown on the Isle of Wight led to a great fondness for paddle steamers. I can still remember views of the great liners like the *Mauretania* and the *Berengaria* as seen from the deck of railway ferries PS *Ryde* or PS *Sandown* as they headed from Portsmouth Harbour to the waiting train on the pier at Ryde. Later I was to travel from London to York via New Holland just to marvel at the skill of the stokers on PS *Wingfield Castle* whose designers had clearly given no thought to the accessibility of the firebox doors.

Back in the 1960s the Caledonian Steam Packet used to invite a few railwaymen who could influence party traffic to spend a few days on the Clyde estuary each September so that they could appreciate what the company's steamer services had to offer. It was a memorable event embracing paddle steamer journeys, tours of the resorts and islands and quite overwhelming hospitality. After breakfast at the hotel another one would appear on the outward steamer journey followed by morning coffee and biscuits and a pre-lunch whisky sampling. A short coach tour before lunch was followed by another hotel showing just what it could serve to impress, both liquid and solid. Finally there was high tea on the return steamer trip and then a gargantuan dinner in the evening. By this time the need for some exercise was imperative and led to an enthusiastic, if rash, participation in the 'Scottish evening' when those who thought that dancing over crossed swords was easy found out the hard way that it was not. Years later another Clyde trip on PS *Caledonia* produced the spectacle of the paddler rescuing passengers from another vessel disabled by a huge jellyfish in the cooling water intake.

Wooden Cobwebs

This was a name given to the wooden viaducts originally provided on the main line west from Saltash Bridge into Cornwall. It derived from the delicate tracery of Baltic pine which surmounted the stone piers of no less than thirty-four viaducts between St Germans and College Wood, near Falmouth.

The Cornwall Railway had a tough time getting its Bill approved by Parliament not least because it originally planned to cross the Hamoaze using a 58ft long boat to transfer trains from one side to the other. In the same rather unreal spirit Sir Charles Napier, for the War Office, wanted the line incorporated in the nation's coastal defences and fortified with Martello towers!

The aftermath of the 1845–46 Railway Mania hit the Cornwall Railway badly forcing it to reduce its capital requirements, abandon planned branches

Early travellers in Cornwall thought these wooden viaducts too flimsy but they had an excellent safety record.

and delay construction work. No longer could it afford conventional masonry viaducts to cross the many deep valleys carrying streams from the moors to Cornwall's south coast. Brunel's solution was to build viaducts with upper works made of relatively cheap yellow pine 'kyanised' to prevent decay and supported by masonry piers some 60ft apart. From these three sets of braced diagonal struts supported the massive beams carrying the decking. The viaduct at St Pinnock rose to a height of 151ft and the one at Truro was 443 yards long.

Disinfecting Plant

Another example of the slightly unusual activities in which railways became involved is the provision of disinfecting equipment. Medical authorities had a right to require any vehicle that might have become infected to be thoroughly sterilised before being returned to service. To do this the Great Western installed an 85ft long air-tight cylinder at Swindon into which could be placed an infected vehicle. Once sealed inside a 28in vacuum was created and the temperature raised to 120 degrees Fahrenheit. This was an effective treatment for vermin and could be supplemented by pumping formaldehyde gas into the cylinder which tackled the infection when the vacuum was broken.

NINETEEN

BYWAYS

From what has gone before it will be crystal clear that beyond the mainstream railway activity there are many curious and intriguing byways. These are just a few of them.

The Carpella Break

For thirteen years, from 16 December 1909 to 18 April 1922, the Great Western Railway had to close the middle section of its line from Burngullow to Drinnick Mill and service it from either end. The 3-mile line involved had originally been opened on 1 July 1869 by the Newquay & Cornwall Junction Railway under the authority of an Act of 1864, had become part of the Cornwall Minerals Railway system in 1874 and then of the GWR from 1896. As was the case with most land sold for early railway construction, the mineral rights remained with the vendor.

The trouble began when the Carpella United Clay Co. wanted to extract china clay in the area through which the line ran. They went to court to establish that they could do this because china clay was a mineral and eventually, on appeal, got a House of Lords ruling to this effect. The GWR now had no alternative but to remove a sixty-two chain section of line from milepost 290, near Foxhole village, and to wait thirteen years before it could be restored. History has labelled the section 'The Carpella Break'.

The Condor

In the 1960s the London Midland Region made a bid to secure more freight traffic between London and Glasgow by introducing a special express freight container service between those two points. It was strongly marketed and given the brand name of the Condor service. Now, quite why the originators of the scheme chose the name of a large

Pictured in 1970 when new rail facilities were opened, Merehead Quarry, although a byway in the heart of Somerset, has despatched thousands of trainloads of stone.

South American vulture for their new service is not clear but it was soon causing consternation among the other railway regions in London.

To maintain loadings on the new service it was aggressively promoted by the LMR salesmen. They were not over-scrupulous about where the traffic came from with the result that other parts of the organisation found its existing and potential business in jeopardy. One line manager was even provoked into referring to the Condor as 'an ugly, bald bird over fond of sticking its beak where it is not wanted'.

Longest Train

In 1968 BR assembled a train of 100 ferry wagons for a Westinghouse P4 air brake trial. The tests took place between Peak Forest and Broadholme on the LMR and at 5,000ft long the train was believed to be the largest train in Europe hauled by a single locomotive.

Stores

Along with most other principal railways the Great Western operated a system of supplying stations with stores using vans attached to laid down services. Each van had an attendant for issuing new items but only against the surrender of the worn-out one. Three movement circuits starting from Swindon enabled the whole system to be covered on a weekly basis. Lamp vans generally carried lamp oil and other inflammable items with other vans circulating with rolling stock spares for shed staff and catering supplies for the various refreshment rooms.

The recording of stores issues was meticulous and their variety extensive. There were, for example, ten different types of brush on offer including ones for 'Stove Polishing' and others for 'Platform Edges' and 'Deck Scrubbing'.

The Live Shell

Railway pioneers came from all walks of life and many were highly colourful characters. At least one was a hero, for the railway built between Cambridge and Bedford owed its existence to an earlier small private line developed by a larger than life figure. He was Sir William Peel VC, the third son of statesman Sir Robert Peel. His early adult life was spent as an officer in the Royal Navy serving all over the world and doing adventurous things like sailing up the Nile and crossing the desert to Khartoum. He earned his Victoria Cross in the Crimean War when he served with the Naval Brigade at the siege of Sebastopol and threw a live shell with the fuse still burning back at the Russians.

Captain Peel then began to implement his plans for a railway from his estate at Potton to Sandy to secure a link with the infant Great Northern main line. A Roman sword was found during the excavations which he had made into a sword for himself and put to good use at the second relief of Lucknow. The railway was completed while Peel was away campaigning and opened by his wife just ten months before her husband's death at Cawnpore in 1858. She adopted the name of Peel's ship *Shannon* for its first engine.

Captain Peel's Railway had four years of independent existence before it was taken over by the Bedford & Cambridge Railway. It was worked with two engines, two wagons, a brake van and a trolley. Using a red flag sufficed for signalling and there was nothing so grand as intermediate stations. Trains just stopped at farmhouses or wherever people wanted to join or alight.

Another Hero

When the 4-mile 624-yard Severn tunnel was opened in 1886 it had taken thirteen years to build, used up 76 million bricks and survived countless crises, particularly various forms of water inundation. Even so the effort and expenditure was hugely worthwhile, especially in shortening the old railway route around the Severn River via Gloucester and thus getting Welsh coal to London and the south more quickly and cheaply.

One of the greatest challenges faced by the tunnel's builders occurred when the Great Spring broke into and flooded the workings. To tackle the huge task of getting the work going again the GWR engaged engineer Thomas Walker to take charge of the operations and he determined that the first task was to close an iron door located about 1,000ft from the bottom of one of the access shafts. This could only be done by a diver of great courage and experience and Walker had such a man in his leading diver whose name was Lambert. Walker's own account of Lambert's first attempt reveals the magnitude of the task:

> He [Lambert] started on his perilous journey armed with only a short iron bar, and carefully groped his way in total darkness over the debris which strewed the bottom of the heading, past upturned skips, tools, and lumps of rock, which had been left in the panic of 1879, until he reached within 100ft from the door, when he found it was impossible to drag the air-hose after him, as it rose to the top of the heading, and its friction against the rock and the head-trees offered greater resistance than he could overcome. He, however, would not give up without an effort, and he pluckily sat down and drew some of the hose to him and then started on again, but after one or two vain efforts he found it impossible to proceed, and was obliged to return to the shaft defeated.

The next stage in the saga is described by another of the engineers:

> He [Lambert] was dreadfully disappointed by his failure; but the Contractor, having heard of the new apparatus for diving without air pipes, which Fleuss, its inventor, was exhibiting daily at the London Aquarium, invited him to come down with his patent apparatus, and close the door.
>
> Fleuss accordingly came there, and went down with Lambert to the mouth of the heading; but when he had groped about and found the sort of place he was expected to go into for nearly a quarter of a mile, his heart failed him and he came up again. He said he would not undertake to go and close the door for ten thousand pounds.

The final act in this saga revealed that Lambert was made of sterner stuff. He volunteered to make one more attempt to close the door by borrowing the Fleuss apparatus which was totally different to anything he had ever come across in that it was self contained with its own air supply. Still in the dark waters, stumbling over debris and knocking himself on the rocky walls of the tunnel, he pushed forward again bravely placing his trust in a completely unfamiliar appliance. Its worst feature was that the nose clip designed to fit its inventor was far too small for Lambert who suffered so severe a headache that he had to turn back and have the clip altered. That done he finally succeeded in closing the door and reducing the raging inflow of water to a level where the pumps could master it.

Prize Fights

Prior to the coming of the railways prize fighting had generally taken place after race meetings or other such gatherings. The Thames steamers did a good business in carrying spectators to see these bare knuckle contests which operated with few rules and went on for round after round until one of the contestants was battered senseless and could not continue.

Although prize fighting was completely illegal many railways were too desperate for revenue to have scruples and proved only too willing to carry huge crowds to secret venues and charge a much higher fare than normal because of the risk involved. The lines radiating from London, especially those serving Kent, laid on quite a few special trains to take the fighters and their supporters to remote destinations particularly in the years up to the early 1860s when the new county police forces were becoming more effective.

The operation of these prize fight specials was an extremely haphazard affair. The need for secrecy meant that very few railway staff knew of the train's existence and the London police habit of stationing a constable at every suburban station pushed the chosen destinations well out into the country, in at least one case onto an abandoned stretch of line. If the police appeared when the fight was in progress the train just moved on to somewhere else!

Chariot Rescue

In 1966 the Area Manager at Evesham received information about a broken rail in the section between Evesham and Pershore. He talked to the local permanent way staff who had a spare rail at their depot but no means of getting it to the site. Another piece of good fortune was the availability of a light diesel locomotive but, unfortunately, there was no suitable wagon to load the rail on.

Improvisation was a notable feature among railwaymen and in this case took the form of using a shunters' truck, nicknamed a 'chariot', and loading the rail onto it.

There was a fearful overhang almost touching the ballast but a red flag was tied on the rear and the train and its scratch crew set off, albeit slowly and gingerly, for the scene of the breakage. They arrived safely, got the spare rail

A typical GWR shunting scene with the shunter riding on his 'Chariot', a vehicle peculiar to the Great Western.

unloaded, cut to length and installed in place of the breakage, all without causing delay to the normal train service.

Elopement Excursions

An enterprising and romantic collaboration between Thomas Cook and the Midland Railway offered to stop their Gloucester to Scotland excursion trains at Gretna Green long enough for couples to marry or, as it was expressed at the time, to enable couples 'to terminate single blessedness'.

'Fixed'

The extensive fleet of vessels operated by the railways played a gallant part in the two world wars either in maintaining the service on important routes or in roles such as troop carriers and minesweepers. There were numerous encounters with the enemy and a fine display of seamanship and bravery from all members of the railway maritime staff.

The SS *Pembroke* was involved in one of the earliest encounters in the First World War when, sailing peacefully back from Guernsey to Weymouth, she was pounced upon by a surfaced submarine which had hidden its silhouette behind a yacht. Sheer speed got the *Pembroke* to safety. Not long afterwards the SS *Ibex* turned the tables on another submarine which appeared out of nowhere on a misty moonlight night. No sooner had the submarine opened fire when the *Ibex* responded with her single gun, scored a direct hit and, as a report recorded, 'fixed her there and then'. The captain and crew of the *Ibex* got an award of £500 from the Admiralty.

The restored
veteran
locomotive
Lion.

Active Retirement

The veteran locomotive *Lion* was built in 1838 for the Liverpool & Manchester
Railway and was pensioned off to a more sedentary life as a stationary steam
plant on the Mersey Docks from 1859 until 1928. It was then restored and took
part in the L&M centenary celebrations, following this with a film career in
Victoria the Great, *The Lady with a Lamp* and *The Titfield Thunderbolt*.

Smashing Success

On 17 October 1848 Boston celebrated the opening of the railway link
between Peterborough and the New Holland–Hull ferry with the usual
marching, speeches and banqueting. But the last train slightly marred the
occasion by running two hours late and smashing through the London
Road crossing gates, the gatekeeper having gone home on time!

Hat and Stick Fares

The Liskeard & Caradon Railway was authorised to carry the copper and
granite mined on Caradon Hill but this did not stop it carrying passengers.
They travelled free but paid, instead, for baskets, hats, sticks, umbrellas and
parcels. Locals were also allowed to use the tracks as a footpath, at their own
risk of course.

TWENTY

LOOKING BACK

In these days of railway sophistication it is not easy to envisage the circumstances surrounding the promotion, construction and operation of the early lines. The only experience available came from building canals, powering the first paddle steamers and agricultural engines and operating a few primitive industrial tramways. Yet, despite this, the courage and foresight of the early pioneers met the immense challenge of quite lengthy routes such as that of the London & Birmingham Railway, the London & Southampton and the Great Western.

For every forward-looking promoter there were several doubters. Some made a career out of their opposition like Colonel Sibthorpe in Parliament and Dr Dionysius Lardner in academic circles but, fortunately for later generations, the pioneers were from a determined mould and succeeded despite the constraints of ill-informed opinion and statutory regulation. Of course, they made mistakes and some of the practices they employed seem odd by today's standards.

Pioneer Engine Driver

Jim Hurst, the first engine driver employed by the Great Western Railway, was born in Lancashire in 1811. He had no schooling and was put to work in a cotton mill at the tender age of nine but later had a spell at the Vulcan Locomotive Works before joining his father as a driver on the Liverpool & Manchester Railway. There he met Daniel Gooch and had to appeal to him for a job after blotting his copybook when his light engine ran into another L&M train.

At the end of 1837 Hurst accompanied two locomotives Gooch had purchased for the GWR from the Vulcan works on their sea journey from Liverpool to London and then by canal to West Drayton. *Vulcan* and *Premier* were then carted by road ready for use on the opening day of the first section of the new railway.

Starting with the 8 a.m. train from Paddington on 4 June 1838 Hurst worked all over the expanding GWR system but his lively temper and equally lively locomotive handling often led him into trouble. In 1842 he refused to work a train because of a dispute over the substitute guard and a year later had to answer a charge of giving footplate rides for a fee. Jim was then dismissed in 1856 for a fight with a porter, but managed to get reinstated. Despite a somewhat turbulent career he stayed with the Great Western until he retired on a pension in 1876.

Off the Road

'Off the Road' has long been the colloquial term for the derailment of an engine, coach or wagon. It may well have been inherited from the stage coach era and was certainly relevant in those early years when the whole business of running trains was so much a matter of trial and error. This much is apparent in the diary record kept by George Gibbs, a prominent Bristol member of the GWR's Bristol Committee of Directors. On 9 January 1838 he recorded:

Another case of 'off the road', this time a shunting mishap on the harbour lines at Bristol.

The engines, after some delay in getting up steam, sallied forth; but the curve in the turn-out proving too sharp for them, they got off the rail two or three times, and it was an hour before they could get them on the main line.

On 7 July 1838:

We went at four o'clock to Paddington, and soon after news was brought us that the 'Vulcan' was off the line and had sunk up to the axle. This led to an accumulation of trains and people, and in the attempt to correct the evil another engine got off the line and sank in the same way....I was so sick of the scene that I made off, finding that I could not be of any use.

Air Services

Using parliamentary powers secured in 1929 the Great Western Railway inaugurated the first railway air service on 12 April 1933. This operated between Plymouth and Cardiff to carry passengers across the natural obstacle of the Bristol Channel and avoid the circuitous rail journey via Bristol. Subsequently the four main line railway companies formed Railway Air Services in association with Imperial Airways and eventually operated de Havilland biplanes over some 5,700 route miles under one title or another.

At this period the aircraft in use might be expected to make a forced landing rather than crash. In the event of engine failure the pilot would look for a good, flat field and gently glide his plane in to achieve a safe if undignified landing. Indeed, the GWR instructions for emergency landings clearly assumed he would be able to 'telephone on landing to the nearest railway station' and get the stationmaster 'to arrange for one or more cars, as required, to proceed to the place where the machine has landed and take the passengers and cargo to the nearest railway station'.

It was not unknown at the time for Imperial Airways pilots to carry a pot of paint with them. This was so that in the event of a forced landing, the company's name on the aeroplane could be painted over to avoid unwelcome publicity.

Specials

At one time the number and variety of special trains was quite incredible. In 1920, for example, two specials conveyed 1,000 East London women to Chingford for an Epping Forest outing. The engine carried a shield and flags, the coaches a large bow in patriotic colours and letters which spelled out 'Good Luck to Horatio' to recognise organiser Horatio Bottomley's generous gesture.

This Carpets Trade special has been painted in a distinctive white livery and provided with a beautifully turned out locomotive.

Exhibition or Show Trains became a tool in the promotional armoury of commerce in the 1930s. A pioneer in this area was HMV who organised a three month national tour to showcase its wireless, radiogram and gramophone products using a train made up of a showroom, a generator van and a dining car converted into a café plus sleeping quarters. The company even persuaded the Prime Minister of the day to send the train on its first journey. One peculiar feature of the launch is described in a press report of the time:

> A little Scottish girl, attired in national costume, armed with a radio valve fixed to a stick and filled with champagne, christened the train by smashing the valve on a gramophone record.

It should be added that the 'gramophone record' was also fixed to a stick projecting from the side of the leading coach of the train!

Decoration

The works at the western end of the original GWR main line were the responsibility of a Bristol committee of its directors. They wanted a railway to be proud of, and even today the stretch of line running through Sidney Gardens at Bath and on to Bristol still displays a number of decorative features.

In 1837 the digging work associated with St Anne's Tunnel unearthed two huge rounded boulders which Brunel happily mounted on pedestals on either side of the eastern portal. There is a story that one of these subsequently fell into the path of a train and cost the life of a quarryman who helped to remove it and avoid a serious accident. A hundred years later the other boulder was offered to Bristol University who accepted and put it on display.

Brunel was also apparently behind another bit of fanciful decoration in the same area. During the construction of a tunnel entrance retaining wall in 1839 a ground movement rendered its completion unnecessary. Brunel thought it looked so like a ruined medieval gateway that he had ivy planted to increase the picturesque effect. A later, less romantic engineer had the ivy removed and the wall profile normalised.

Copying

Typewriters and carbon paper may have been on the scene before the end of the nineteenth century but they took a long while to become commonplace in railway offices. Before they did copying accounts and similar documents required a heavy press and a huge bound book similar in size to the traditional family bible. The book had fifty or so lined pages in the front for creating an index of the copies 'pressed' onto the many flimsy sheets at the rear. The copying process then involved dampening one of these sheets, placing the account document upon it and squeezing the lot with the press. As in other such matters practice made perfect but until it did either the ink of the original got smudged, it failed to record clearly or the original just got stuck to the page it was supposed to be copied on.

Early Rules and Procedures

Those who worked for Robert Stephenson & Co. in 1838 had to sign a list of twenty-two rules and regulations before being employed in the company's works. Any breaches of these rules resulted in fines which were deducted from wages and handed over to the Sick Fund. The dearest fine was the one shilling levied for transgressions like 'smoking in the Manufactory' or 'creating a tumult or noise' there. Waste and damage were similarly penalised with a shilling again being deducted from 'any Workman leaving his Candle burning or neglecting to shut his Gas Cock'.

Twenty-five years later the MS&L Rule Book also included some rather odd statements, including a requirement for stationmasters and clerks-in-charge to sand the rails for 20–30 yards from the station platforms. Guards were ordered not to pass over the tops of carriages without 'urgent necessity' and porters had to 'observe the indication of any passengers that may desire to alight by their knocking at the windows or otherwise'. Stations were told that they must always be ready to receive special trains without prior notice and that 'no excuse of want of notice will ever be accepted in the event of an accident'.

Chicanery

The early railways were not without their shady deals. They were pretty speculative ventures anyway and it is less than surprising that some of the people involved were not above one form of irregularity or another.

When the Great Grimsby & Sheffield Junction Railway was authorised in 1845 its proposed lines included one from Brocklesby to New Holland on the south bank of the Humber estuary. Cunningly a group of GG&SJ directors bought up the Humber Ferry Company for £10,300 and, less than a year later, sold it to the main company for twice that amount. They had clearly seen that the new railway would need a link across the river to Hull and made a cool 100 per cent profit out of their foresight.

Interestingly the north bank terminus of the ferry route at Corporation Pier was another ticket issuing station which never had any trains.

Cotswold Pioneer

As early as 1821 Parliament authorised a 17-mile tramway between Stratford-on-Avon and Moreton-in-the-Marsh which opened in 1826. A 2-mile branch to Shipston-on-Stour was approved later and opened in 1836. In its early years this was a horse-worked line with some peculiar traffic arrangements which included a local publican operating a passenger vehicle on the line and traders hauling their own goods traffic, sometimes with a passenger or two in the same waggon.

A contemporary account by one early passenger gives a graphic picture of travelling on the tramway:

> The journey was performed outside an ordinary railway carriage, which had been adapted to the necessities of horse traction. It was fitted with a box for the driver, and seats beside him for passengers. Attached to the carriage in front was a platform, on which the sagacious horse mounted when it had

A reminder of
the Stratford and
Moreton Tramway, in
the form of this old
wagon, is preserved
beside the river at
Stratford-on-Avon.

drawn clear of our carriage at the top of an incline, thus escaping being
tripped up as we descended at a rattling good speed. The Inspectors of the
Board of Trade not having discovered this tramway, the occurrence or non-
occurrence of accidents was left chiefly to the goodness of Providence. When
we came to the foot of the incline, the guard applied his brake as tightly as
he could; we all, to the best of our individual capacities, held on to our seats
and, if we had taken firm hold, we thus managed to avoid being pitched off
head-foremost. When the carriage came to a stand, the horse dismounted
and drew us along as before.

There was a tunnel, too, on approaching which the driver was kind enough
to suggest that such of the outside passengers as thought it likely they would
have any further use for their brains, should duck their heads as low as possible
and carry their hats in their hands.

Alarming Riot

Under this heading a *Times* reporter filed a lurid account of a confrontation
which took place in 1851 during the construction of Mickleton Tunnel on
the section of the Oxford, Worcester & Wolverhampton (OW&W) Railway
line between Honeybourne and Moreton-in-the-Marsh. The whole project
had been bedevilled by a shortage of funds and when the tunnel contractor,
one Marchant, fell behind on his section this just delayed opening, and
earning some revenue, even further. Brunel, as the OW&W engineer,
ordered Marchant to leave and arranged for another contractor, Peto &

Betts, to take over the unfinished section. But Marchant refused to evacuate his men and 'a slight skirmish' took place.

Not the most patient of men, Brunel promptly used an intervening weekend to bring in a large force of navvies from other areas in order to dispossess the recalcitrant Marchant. They marched through the night in order to get onto the tunnel site early on the Monday but before they attained their objective matters got somewhat out of hand, as the newspaper report recorded:

On reaching the Worcester end of the tunnel Mr Cowdery with his gang of 200 men from Evesham and Wyre was met by Mr Marchant who dared anyone of Peto & Betts men to pass the bridge on pain of being shot, Mr Marchant himself being well supplied with pistols. Mr Cowdery, exercising great forebearance at the unseemly conduct of Mr Marchant, told his men on no account whatsoever to strike a blow. Mr Cowdery, finding that all expostulation was useless and Mr Brunel giving a peremptory order for Messrs Peto & Betts men to proceed and take everything in the line, a rush was made to the men which after a few seconds was repelled with great force by Marchant and his men, the consequence was that several heads were broken and three men had their shoulders dislocated. Up to this time the navvies had not called into requisition the picks or pickaxes or shovels, but a man in the employ of Marchant having drawn pistols he was seized upon and his skull nearly severed in two.

This occurrence for a time daunted Marchant, and he left Messrs Peto & Betts men for an hour in undisputed possession of the ground. At the expiration of that time he returned with some three dozen policemen from the Gloucester Constabulary and some privates of the Gloucester Artillery accompanied by two magistrates of the place, who immediately commenced reading the Riot Act. At this junction a melee had taken place on a high embankment and here several broken limbs had been a result of the conflict. About 2 o'clock Mr Charles Watson of Warwick arrived with upwards of 200 men, and the Great Western company who sent a similar number in order to assist them.

Marchant, now finding that all attempts at resistance were useless, from the vast majority in numbers of his opponents, gave in, and he and Mr Brunel adjourned, in order to come to acceptable arrangement. In their absence a small bunch of navvies again met and one of them had his little finger bitten off, another his head severely wounded. Eventually it was arranged that Messrs Cubitt and Stephenson were to be arbitrators and that the works were to be suspended for a fortnight.

TWENTY-ONE

JUST DIFFERENT

Some things are just so different that they defy classification.

Railway Castles

Railways have connections with several castles, including their ownership of Sandgate Castle in Kent where the Southern Railway used to charge 3*d* a head for summer visitors to the site. The station at Berwick-on-Tweed on the East Coast Main Line has a plaque on which the following words are displayed between the coats of arms of England and Scotland:

> The station stands on the site of the Great Hall of Berwick Castle. Here on the 17th November 1292 the claim of Robert Bruce to the crown of Scotland was declined and the decision in favour of John Baliol was given by King Edward I before the full Parliament of England and a large gathering of the nobility and populace of both England and Scotland.

Walking Sticks

Three lucky railwaymen received walking sticks to mark a narrow escape they had on 18 December 1879. This was the date of the Tay Bridge disaster and the three, a driver, fireman and guard, would have been on the ill-fated train that plunged from the broken bridge had they not spent overlong in the local hostelry when their shift ended. To mark their good fortune each was presented with an inscribed walking stick made from wood recovered from the carriages of the disaster train.

Another unusual walking stick has acted as the informal 'badge of office' of successive chief civil engineers of the GWR and BR(W). It originally belonged to Brunel and was hinged in three sections which could be opened out after removing the handle and ferrule. When opened the stick was exactly 7ft ¼in long, the width of his beloved broad gauge.

Permanent Way

Ordinary railway trackwork is complicated enough and it was even worse during the period when the Great Western was using the mixed gauge over some of its routes. Perhaps one of the greatest of railway civil engineering feats was the final elimination of the broad gauge in 1892 in a mammoth exercise involving 4,000 men labouring on 171 miles of railway to effect the change to standard gauge with the minimum of disruption to traffic.

A lot of work was done in readiness for the hours of conversion especially in getting tools and equipment in place and cutting sleepers and rails to the right length. The men were brought down in special trains in the days immediately preceding conversion along with the narrow gauge stock required for the services on Monday 23 May. The previous Friday the last broad gauge train from Cornwall brought out all the coaches and wagons still on hand in the south-west with every station having to certify that it was clear of such items. Those engines not being re-gauged and the redundant wagons and coaches finished up in a 'graveyard' at Swindon, a sight which would have brought Brunel to tears.

Nowadays the railway track is highly sophisticated with high quality, long-welded rails, sophisticated chairs and sleepers, expansion joints, motors to operate points, interlocking to prevent unwanted movement and rigorous

A picture of the gauge conversion work at Plymouth in May 1892.

and regular inspection. Even so some highly complex layouts remain necessary at busy spots and the few non-standard situations include tracks which cross at right angles.

Secret Trains

At least three trains were fitted out in the early 1960s for use in emergencies and then spent the next twenty years strategically stabled in remote locations and, thankfully, unused. Two three-coach units of Hastings stock were stored near Tunbridge Wells West and Faversham stations with another eleven specially fitted vehicles kept in readiness near Church Stretton. The coaches were provided with generating plant and special telecommunications equipment which could be plugged into the main telephone network in the event of an emergency and thus permit the control of any special rail movements required.

Railway Time

For many years the ten o'clock time signal passed between railway locations was the basis for displacing local time with the common use of Greenwich time. However, it did not become universal until every railway had completed its installation of the electric telegraph so more reliable arrangements had to be used in certain special cases. One of these was introduced when the Irish Mail began running on 1 August 1848 when a carefully adjusted watch, in its own leather case, travelled with each train. An Admiralty messenger brought the watch to Euston each day and handed it to the guard of the train. On arrival at Holyhead he, in turn, notified an officer from the Kingstown boat of the exact time and then brought the watch back with him to London. The practice continued for over ninety years, long after the original need for it had disappeared.

Very Nearly

In 1911 the North Eastern Railway secured an Act of Parliament authorising the 3.5-mile Seaton Sluice branch to serve a little seaside village of that name to the north of Whitley Bay. Construction was nearing completion when war broke out and construction work duly ceased. A rail-mounted gun did operate on some temporary track but the project was dropped after the war and the works either abandoned or demolished. Not seeing Seaton Sluice as a name to entice visitors the NER had planned to call its station there Collywell Bay, which had a much better ring.

Bonus Mileages

In the days when railway charges were based on distances you could buy *Railway Mileage Tables* to work out your own costs. The data even embraced those cases where a railway was allowed to charge extra as recompense for higher construction costs. Examples of these included the Forth Bridge where the LNER could charge local traffic for an extra 10 miles and add 19 miles for longer distance movements. Over its inner area routes the Metropolitan Railway could charge three times the actual distance and the Great Western got an allowance of 12 miles for the 4.4 of the Severn Tunnel. Other such locations included Shildon Tunnel and the incline from Cowlairs to Glasgow Queen Street.

Stations

London's St Pancras is again in the forefront of railway development as the new home for the accelerated Eurostar services. Curiously the design of the original St Pancras is founded on, of all things, a standard beer barrel. To allow the approach route to cross the Regent's Canal the terminus had to be raised 17ft above Euston Road which created a space below the platforms ideal for receiving and storing loads of Burton beer. To accommodate the highest possible number of barrels the ideal distance between supports was found to be 29ft 4ins. This and the use of columns and girders instead of the brick piers originally intended influenced the whole design and appearance of the station.

Extra space was added to Shrewsbury station by raising the original building and adding a new floor at ground level.

Railways in the Community

The link between railways and the community is well known in the case of the various 'railway towns' but there were quite a few less dramatic instances of such paternalism as well. At lonely Gorton on the West Highland line, for example, the LMS provided an old coach body to serve as a school classroom for pupils who could not be accommodated at the school at Rannoch.

The North British Railway also took good care of isolated communities like the one which embraced its staff at the remote Riccarton Junction. It provided housing, a shop and post office, and a school there, and even brought in a doctor by light engine in cases of emergency. For the spiritual welfare of its employees the company ran a free church train on Sundays, taking staff to the kirk at Hawick one week and to church or chapel at Newcastleton the next.

Sheriff's Crossing

Since the Middle Ages the sheriff of Lichfield had ridden the city boundaries each year on horseback and from 1848 the route had included a railway crossing between the Lichfield City and Trent Valley stations. With the coming of electrification horses were banned from crossing the line but the sheriff avoided any problems by accepting a BR payment of £200 to buy out the right and donating the money to charity.

The Lie Sheet

This was the colloquial name for the Half Yearly Certificate that every stationmaster and goods agent had to sign to confirm that all the premises and every piece of equipment were in good order. Since proper inspection of everything was just not possible signing for some items tended to be a formality. Bill Bradshaw, when goods agent at Oxford, had been urged not to enquire about two bicycles shown on the return, just to sign that they were on the depot and used only for official business. Unable to resist the urge to find out the true situation he insisted on seeing the machines. A shed was unlocked for him and revealed two aged brown machines which clearly, to quote him, 'had not been ridden in years and were never likely to see the road again'. It had just been easier for everyone to complete the lie sheet than go through the lengthy process of disposing of the unwanted and unloved cycles.

Tongue in Cheek

One peer of the realm made so many complaints of his experiences in moving himself and his racehorses around the railway system that he warranted a separate file in the correspondence office. One particularly vituperative letter ended with a postscript deploring the untidy state of Birmingham Snow Hill station and its refreshment rooms. The reply assured him of management's desire to keep stations clean and tidy and regretted the unfortunate lapse on the occasion in question, ascribing it to the fact that there had been a race meeting at Wolverhampton and adding, 'as your Lordship will appreciate, racegoers attracted by such events are disorderly and untidy people with little consideration for other travellers'. However much the habits of race crowds may have contributed to the complainant's problem this was not the wisest of remarks and attracted a rejoinder which began 'As Chairman of Wolverhampton Racecourse…'

The First Train

When the very first train ran on a certain line in Norfolk the oldest inhabitant was sent to see it and report back to the villagers who were not able to leave their work in the fields. He was directed to a vantage point just before a short tunnel and duly took up his position. Back in the village inn that evening he was asked to say what he thought of the train. After a pause for thought he said, 'Well bor, Oi can't tell ya for sarten cos thet come rushen round the bend and when thet see me thet wholly shruck and rushed inta a burrer.'

The Selection Process

Before the days of group interviews and psychometric testing Hugh Jenkins had worked hard to prepare himself for his first interview for a Traffic Apprentice position. This took place before a Regional Panel who warned him of the 'deep and searching interview' which would take place before the National Panel at BRB headquarters. Meanwhile the chairman said they just needed to see what sort of chap he was and asked Hugh for his opinion on the current state of Welsh rugby.

At the next stage the chairman of the National Panel told him that since he had already been subject to a 'deep and searching interview' at regional level they could concentrate on finding out what sort of chap he was. Did he, for example, have any views on the state of Welsh Rugby!

Reserve Funds

At one of the Potteries stations the Monday morning check of the left luggage lockers found them all empty except one which contained a solitary pound note. Puzzled, the staff paid the amount into petty cash. Later that day a member of HM Forces complained of finding his locker empty of the pound he had left there to ensure that he was not totally broke at the end of his weekend leave.

In Memorium

As in every other walk of life, railways have their sad links with death. Memorial tablets still exist at several stations recording the names of railwaymen who died on war service. By an unhappy irony Field Marshal Sir Henry Wilson MP who unveiled the 1,220-name memorial at Liverpool Street on 22 June 1922 was assassinated on the doorstep of his home just a short time later.

Even more remarkable was the death of twenty-four-year-old Henry West on Reading station just six days before it opened on 30 March 1840. The cause? A whirlwind!

Coupling

Using a long pole with a hook at the end to lift a heavy railway wagon coupling, guide it onto another wagon's coupling hook just at the right moment and then extract the shunting pole from between the newly linked vehicles is an acquired skill. With years of practice many shunters became incredibly proficient and sometimes put their prowess to the test in local coupling contests.

Such contests were very popular on the former North Eastern Railway and in one contest at Hull in 1911 the winner coupled and uncoupled twenty-one wagons in a fraction over two minutes and was rewarded with the prize of a tea service. Even the slowest of the forty-eight entrants took only 3 minutes 10 seconds. There had been even better performances at Spalding in 1890 when a local shunter coupled and uncoupled a twenty-wagon rake in 1 minute 46 seconds and a Peterborough guard came first in the fifteen-wagon section with a time of 1 minute 16 seconds.

The Unloved Railway

A prime candidate for this title was the Eastern Counties Railway (ECR) which planned to build a trunk route from London to Norwich and in June

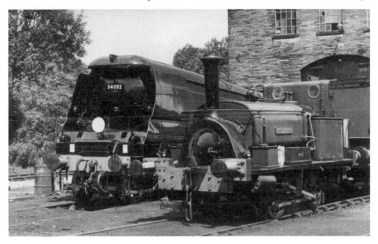

Two contrasting locomotives but each has a substantial coupling, that of the streamlined
SR No.34092 of the screw type and with vacuum and train heating pipes alongside.

1839 opened the first section of this from a station at Devonshire Street, Mile
End to Romford. Despite the attendant celebrations it then took the ECR
another five years to get as far as Colchester. The link on to Norwich was left
to another company, the Eastern Union with the ECR managing a different
route to Norfolk by leasing one line and taking over another. The company
then bullied a number of smaller concerns into leases and acquisitions that
rarely reflected anything like their original capital costs.

By the 1850s the Eastern Counties Railway had a fairly extensive network
in East Anglia but had a very poor reputation. Its fares were too high, its
punctuality poor and its safety record quite frightening. In 1856 a sarcastic
public notice to passengers pointed out that the ECR trains did offer special
advantages to nervous passengers as they ran so slowly. The final paragraph
of the notice read:

> The Season Tickets may be 10 or 20 per cent. higher than on other Lines,
> but as the time allowed for seeing the country is so liberal on the part of the
> Company, the Passengers must not complain. Railway Companies cannot
> afford to waste Time and Steam without being paid for it.

If you are interested in purchasing other books published by Tempus,
or in case you have difficulty finding any Tempus books in your local bookshop,
you can also place orders directly through our website

www.tempus-publishing.com